Student Activities Manual

for

Adler, Proctor, and Towne's

Looking Out/Looking In

Eleventh Edition

Mary O. Wiemann
Santa Barbara City College

THOMSON
™
WADSWORTH

Australia • Canada • Mexico • Singapore • Spain • United Kingdom • United States

Printer: Darby Printing

0-534-63631-4

For more information about our products, contact us at:
Thomson Learning Academic Resource Center
1-800-423-0563

For permission to use material from this text or product, submit a request online at
http://www.thomsonrights.com
Any additional questions about permissions can be submitted at
thomsonrights@thomson.com

Thomson Wadsworth
10 Davis Drive
Belmont, CA 94002-3098
USA

Asia
Thomson Learning
5 Shenton Way #01-01
UIC Building
Singapore 068808

Australia/New Zealand
Thomson Learning
102 Dodds Street
Southbank, Victoria 3006
Australia

Canada
Nelson
1120 Birchmount Road
Toronto, Ontario M1K 5G4
Canada

Europe/Middle East/South Africa
Thomson Learning
High Holborn House
50/51 Bedford Row
London WC1R 4LR
United Kingdom

Latin America
Thomson Learning
Seneca, 53
Colonia Polanco
11560 Mexico D.F.
Mexico

Spain/Portugal
Paraninfo
Calle/Magallanes, 25
28015 Madrid, Spain

CONTENTS

PREFACE   IX

CHAPTER 1 A FIRST LOOK AT INTERPERSONAL RELATIONSHIPS   1
OUTLINE   1
KEY TERMS   2
ACTIVITIES   3

◆   1.1   Communication Skills Inventory (Invitation to Insight)   3

◆   1.2   Expanding Your Communication Effectiveness (Invitation to Insight) 5

◆❖   1.3   Recognizing Relational Messages (Skill Builder) 7

❖   1.4   Mediated Messages – Channels   (Group Discussion)   9

❖   1.5   Your Call – Communication Basics (Group Discussion)   11

◆❖   1.6   Dear Professor – Relational Responses   (Invitation to Insight/Group Discussion)   13

STUDY GUIDE   15
Crossword Puzzle   15
True/False Questions   16
Completion   18
Multiple Choice Questions   19
Study Guide Answers   21

CHAPTER 2 COMMUNICATION AND IDENTITY: THE SELF AND MESSAGES   23
OUTLINE   23
KEY TERMS   24
ACTIVITIES   25

◆   2.1   Who Do You Think You Are? (Invitation to Insight)   25

◆   2.2   Self-Concept Inventory (Invitation to Insight)   27

◆   2.3   Ego Boosters and Busters (Invitation to Insight)   31

◆   2.4   Reevaluating Your "Can'ts" (Invitation to Insight)   35

◆   2.5   Success in Managing Impressions (Skill Builder)   39

◆   2.6   Mediated Messages—Identity Management (Group Discussion)   41

❖   2.7   Your Call—Identity Management (Group Discussion)   43

◆❖   2.8   Dear Professor—Relational Responses   (Invitation to Insight/Group Discussion)   45

STUDY GUIDE   47
Crossword Puzzle   47
True/False Questions   48
Completion   50
Multiple Choice Questions   50
Study Guide Answers   53

CHAPTER 3 PERCEPTION: WHAT YOU SEE IS WHAT YOU GET   55

     OUTLINE   55
     KEY TERMS   56
     ACTIVITIES   53

◆   3.1   Guarding Against Perceptual Errors (Invitation to Insight)   57

◆   3.2   Examining Your Interpretations (Invitation to Insight)   59

◆   3.3   Shifting Perspectives (Pillow Method) (Invitation to Insight)   65

❖   3.4   Observation and Perception (Skill Builder)   67

❖   3.5   Perception-Checking Practice (Skill Builder)   71

❖   3.6   Perception-Checking (Oral Skill)   75

◆❖   3.7   Mediated Messages—Perception   77

◆❖   3.8   Your Call—Perception   79

◆❖   3.9   Dear Professor—Relational Responses   (Invitation to Insight/Group Discussion)   81

     STUDY GUIDE   83
        Crossword Puzzle   83
        True/False Questions   84
        Completion 86
        Multiple Choice Questions   86
        Study Guide Answers   89

CHAPTER 4 EMOTIONS: THINKING FEELING AND COMMUNICATING   91

     OUTLINE   91
     KEY TERMS   92
     ACTIVITIES   93

❖   4.1   The Components of Emotion (Skill Builder)   93

❖   4.2   Find the Feelings (Skill Builder)   95

❖   4.3   Stating Emotions Effectively (Skill Builder) 9

❖   4.4   Self-Talk (Skill Builder)   101

❖   4.5   Disputing Irrational Thoughts (Invitation to Insight)   105

◆   4.6   Mediated Messages—Expressing Emotion (Group Discussion)   107

◆   4.7   Your Call—Expressing Emotion (Group Discussion)   109

◆❖   4.8   Dear Professor—Relational Responses   (Invitation to Insight/Group Discussion)   111

     STUDY GUIDE   113
        Crossword Puzzle   113
        True/False Questions   114
        Completion   116
        Multiple Choice Questions   117
        Study Guide Answers   119

CHAPTER 5 LANGUAGE: BARRIER AND BRIDGE   121

OUTLINE   121
KEY TERMS   122
ACTIVITIES   123

❖ 5.1   Misunderstood Language (Skill Builder)   123

❖ 5.2   Behavioral Language (Skill Builder) 127

❖ 5.3   Responsible Language (Skill Builder) 129

◆❖ 5.4   "I" Language (Oral Skill)   133

❖ 5.5   Effective Language (Invitation to Insight)   135

◆❖ 5.6   Mediated Messages—Language (Group Discussion)   139

❖ 5.7   Your Call—Language (Group Discussion)   141

◆❖ 5.8   Dear Professor—Relational Responses (Invitation to Insight/Group Discussion)   143

STUDY GUIDE   145
Crossword Puzzle   145
True/False Questions   146
Completion   148
Multiple Choice Questions   149
Study Guide Answers   151

CHAPTER 6 NONVERBAL COMMUNICATION: MESSAGES BEYOND WORDS   153

OUTLINE   153
KEY TERMS   154
ACTIVITIES   155

❖ 6.1   Describing Nonverbal States (Skill Builder)   155

❖ 6.2   Nonverbal How-To's (Skill Builder) 159

◆ 6.3   Evaluating Ambiguity (Invitation to Insight)   161

◆❖ 6.4   Mediated Messages—Nonverbal (Group Discussion) 165

◆ 6.5   Your Call—Nonverbal Behavior (Group Discussion)   167

◆❖ 6.6   Dear Professor—Relational Responses (Invitation to Insight/Group Discussion)   169

STUDY GUIDE   171
Crossword Puzzle   171
True/False Questions   172
Completion   174
Multiple Choice Questions   175
Study Guide Answers   177

CHAPTER 7 LISTENING: MORE THAN MEETS THE EAR   179

    OUTLINE 179
    KEY TERMS 180
    ACTIVITIES   181

◆   7.1   Listening Diary (Invitation to Insight) 181

❖   7.2   Effective Questioning (Skill Builder) 183

◆❖ 7.3   Paraphrasing (Skill Builder) 185

❖   7.4   Listening Choices (Skill Builder) 189

❖   7.5   Informational Listening (Skill Builder) 193

❖   7.6   Listening and Responding Styles (Oral Skill) 195

❖   7.7   Mediated Messages—Listening (Group Discussion) 197

❖   7.8   Your Call--Listening (Group Discussion) 199

◆❖ 7.9   Dear Professor—Relational Responses (Invitation to Insight/Group Discussion) 201

    STUDY GUIDE   203
        Crossword Puzzle   203
        True/False Questions   204
        Completion   205
        Multiple Choice Questions   206
        Study Guide Answers   209

CHAPTER 8 COMMUNICATION AND RELATIONAL DYNAMICS 211

    OUTLINE   211
    KEY TERMS   212
    ACTIVITIES   213

◆   8.1   Discovering Dialectics (Invitation to Insight) 213

❖   8.2   Relational Stages (Invitation to Insight)   215

◆   8.3   Breadth and Depth of Relationships (Invitation to Insight)   219

◆   8.4   Reasons for Nondisclosure (Invitation to Insight)   221

◆   8.5   Degrees of Self-Disclosure (Skill Builder)   223

❖   8.6   Disclosure and Alternatives (Skill Builder)   227

❖   8.7   Mediated Messages—Relational Dynamics (Group Discussion)   231

❖   8.8   Your Call—Relational Dynamics (Group Discussion) 233

◆❖ 8.9   Dear Professor—Relational Responses (Invitation to Insight/Group Discussion) 235

    STUDY GUIDE   237
        Crossword Puzzle   237
        True/False Questions   238
        Completion   241
        Multiple Choice Questions   242
        Study Guide Answers   243

CHAPTER 9 IMPROVING COMMUNICATION CLIMATES 245

OUTLINE 245
KEY TERMS 246
ACTIVITIES 247

◆ 9.1 Understanding Defensive Responses (Invitation to Insight) 247
◆❖ 9.2 Defensive and Supportive Language (Skill Builder) 251
◆❖ 9.3 Writing Clear Messages (Skill Builder) 255
❖ 9.4 Nondefensive Responses to Criticism (Skill Builder) 259
❖ 9.5 Coping with Criticism (Oral Skill) 261
❖ 9.6 Mediated Messages—Climate (Group Discussion) 263
❖ 9.7 Your Call—Climate (Group Discussion) 265
◆❖ 9.8 Dear Professor—Relational Responses (Invitation to Insight/Group Discussion) 267

STUDY GUIDE 269
Crossword Puzzle 269
True/False Questions 270
Completion 272
Multiple Choice Questions 273
Study Guide Answers 275

CHAPTER 10 MANAGING INTERPERSONAL CONFLICTS 277

OUTLINE 277
KEY TERMS 278
ACTIVITIES 279

◆❖ 10.1 Understanding Conflict Styles (Skill Builder) 279
◆ 10.2 Your Conflict Styles (Invitation to Insight) 285
◆❖ 10.3 The End vs. The Means (Invitation to Insight) 289
◆❖ 10.4 Win–Win Problem Solving (Invitation to Insight) 291
❖ 10.5 Conflict Resolution Dyads (Oral Skill) 295
❖ 10.6 Mediated Messages—Conflict Management (Group Discussion) 297
❖ 10.7 Your Call—Conflict Management (Group Discussion) 299
◆❖ 10.8 Dear Professor—Relational Responses (Invitation to Insight/Group Discussion) 301

STUDY GUIDE 303
Crossword Puzzle 303
True/False Questions 304
Completion 305
Multiple Choice Questions 306
Study Guide Answers 309

PREFACE

Welcome to the *Student Activities Manual* for *Looking Out/Looking In*, Eleventh Edition. Responding to feedback from *Activities Manual* users around the country, this *Student Activities Manual* is designed to enhance student learning. The *Student Activities Manual* contains more than 50 class-tested exercises and more than 500 study test items designed to build understanding of principles and proficiency in skills introduced in the text.

Each chapter in the *Student Activities Manual* parallels the chapter in *Looking Out/Looking In*. The following areas in each chapter combine to provide a thorough, student-centered learning package:

•**Outlines** Extended outlines of each chapter begin each section. Many instructors ask students to use the outlines as a lecture guide in class or a place to take notes as they read the chapter.

•**Activities** Students who complete the activities in this workbook will develop understanding and skill in each area through a choice of exercises. Exercises are coded with icons to help you choose how to use them. ❖ denotes a group activity. ◆ identifies an individual one.

Skill Builder activities—designed primarily to help students identify the target behavior in a number of common interpersonal communication situations. These are frequently group activities that reinforce learning in the classroom. They can be done as individual activities.

Invitation to Insight activities—designed to help students discover how newly learned principles can be applied in their everyday lives. They can be grouped together to form a "Communication Journal" for the entire course. While these activities are usually designed for individual use, they can provide the structure for small group discussion or lecture/discussion.

Oral Skill activities—designed to allow students to actually exhibit communication behaviors they have studied. They are designed for individual, dyadic, or small group use in a classroom or lab setting.

Mediated Communication activities—designed to challenge students to apply interpersonal communication principles to the many mediated contexts they encounter. They are designed for individual, dyadic, or small group use in a classroom or lab setting.

Your Call activities—designed to prompt analysis and ethical choices among students. They are designed primarily for group discussion in a classroom or lab setting.

Dear Professor letters and responses—designed to provide communication advice for common relational problems and to apply terms and concepts to life situations. They are designed primarily for both individual reflection and group discussion.

Many of the activities can be used in a variety of ways. Instructors can adapt them, use some or all, grade them or leave them ungraded, assign them as out-of-class exercises, or use them as class enrichment. Student observations in many exercises will lead to class discussions on how to apply the newly learned principles in the "real world" of one's interpersonal relationships.

While they almost always stimulate class discussion, the activities in this manual are designed to do more than keep a class busy or interested. If they are used regularly, they will help students to move beyond simply understanding the principles of interpersonal communication and actually to perform more effectively in a variety of communication situations.

• **Study Guide.** Designed to help students identify major concepts or skills contained in the chapter, these are designed to be done individually, in groups, or with the entire class. Answer keys for all the study guide activities are found at the end of each chapter. Crossword Puzzle, Matching, True/False, Completion, and Multiple Choice items review and reinforce for students as they work at their own pace.

The *Student Activities Manual* should help develop more effective communication, both in class and in students' lives outside the classroom. Students who go through the outlines, fill in the key terms, and complete the study guides do better on quizzes and tests than those who fail to complete some or all of these aids. The greatest satisfaction, however, comes from using the activities in this manual to develop more effective communication with loved ones, co-workers and friends.

Mary Wiemann

CHAPTER ONE

A FIRST LOOK AT INTERPERSONAL RELATIONSHIPS

OUTLINE

Use this outline to take notes as you read the chapter in the text and/or as your instructor lectures in class.

I. **INTRODUCTION TO INTERPERSONAL COMMUNICATION**
   A. **Communication Is Important**
   B. **We Communicate to Satisfy Needs**
      1. Physical needs
      2. Identity needs
      3. Social needs
         a. Pleasure
         b. Affection
         c. Companionship
         d. Escape
         e. Relaxation
         f. Control
      4. Practical goals
         a. Instrumental goals
            1) Get others to behave in ways we want
            2) Career success
         b. Maslow's basic needs
            1) Physical
            2) Safety
            3) Social
            4) Self-esteem
            5) Self-actualization

II. **THE PROCESS OF COMMUNICATION**
   A. **A Linear View**
      1. Sender
      2. Encodes
      3. Message
      4. Channel
      5. Decodes
      6. Receiver
      7. Noise - external

A Transactional View
      1. Environments
      2. Noise
         a. External
         b. Physiological
         c. Psychological

3. Transactional communication is *with* others
4. Definition

III. **COMMUNICATION PRINCIPLES AND MISCONCEPTIONS**
   A. **Communication Principles**
      1. Communication can be intentional or unintentional
      2. It's impossible not to communicate
      3. Communication is irreversible
      4. Communication is unrepeatable
   B. **Communication Misconceptions**
      1. Meanings are not in words
      2. Successful communication doesn't always involve shared understanding
      3. More communication is not always better
      4. No single person or event causes another's reaction
      5. Communication will not solve all problems

IV. **THE NATURE OF INTERPERSONAL COMMUNICATION**
   A. **Two Views of Interpersonal Communication**
      1. Quantitative—dyadic
      2. Qualitative
         a. Uniqueness – rules and roles
         b. Irreplaceability
         c. Interdependence
         d. Disclosure
         e. Intrinsic rewards
         f. Scarcity

Technology and Interpersonal Communication
  1. CMC is computer mediated communication
  2. CMC can increase the quantity and quality of interpersonal communication
  C. Personal and Impersonal Communication: A Matter of Balance

V. COMMUNICATING ABOUT RELATIONSHIPS
  A. Content and Relational Messages
  B. Types of Relational Messages
    1. Affinity
    2. Immediacy
    3. Respect
    4. Control
      a. Decisional
      b. Conversational
  C. Metacommunication

VI. WHAT MAKES AN EFFECTIVE COMMUNICATOR?
  A. Communication Competence Defined
    1. There is no "ideal" way to communicate
    2. Competence is situational
    3. Competence is relational
    4. Competence can be learned
  B. Gender and Communication Competence
  C. Characteristics of Competent Communicators
    1. A wide range of behaviors
    2. The ability to choose the most appropriate behavior
      a. Context
      b. Your goal
      c. Your knowledge of the other person
    3. Skill at performing behaviors
      a. Beginning awareness
      b. Awkwardness
      c. Skillfulness
      d. Integration
    4. Cognitive complexity
    5. Empathy
    6. Self-monitoring
    7. Commitment
      a. Commitment to the other person
      b. Commitment to the message

KEY TERMS

affinity
channel
cognitive complexity
communication
communication competence
computer-mediated communication (CMC)
content message
control (conversational and decision)
decoding
dyad
encoding
environment
immediacy
instrumental goals

interpersonal communication (quantitative and qualitative)
linear communication model
message
meta communication
noise (external, physiological, psychological) receiver
relational message
respect
self-monitoring
sender
transactional communication model
impersonal communication

ACTIVITIES

1.1 COMMUNICATION SKILLS INVENTORY

◆ **Activity Type: Invitation to Insight**

Purposes

1. To discover how satisfied you are with the way you communicate in various situations.
2. To preview some topics that will be covered in *Looking Out/Looking In.*

Instructions

1. Below you will find several communication-related situations. As you read each item, imagine yourself in that situation.
2. For each instance, answer the following question: *How satisfied am I with the way I would behave in this situation and ones like it?* You can express your answers by placing one of the following numbers in the space by each item:

5 = Completely satisfied with my probable action
4 = Generally, though not totally, satisfied with my probable action
3 = About equally satisfied and dissatisfied with my probable action
2 = Generally, though not totally, dissatisfied with my probable action
1 = Totally dissatisfied with my probable action

_____   1. A new acquaintance has just shared some personal experiences with you that make you think you'd like to develop a closer relationship. You have experienced the same things and are now deciding whether to reveal these personal experiences. (8)

_____   2. You've become involved in a political discussion with someone whose views are the complete opposite of yours. The other person asks, "Can't you at least understand why I feel as I do?" (3, 7)

_____   3. You are considered a responsible adult by virtually everyone except one relative who still wants to help you make all your decisions. You value your relationship with this person, but you need to be seen as more independent. You know you should do something about this situation. (9, 10)

_____   4. In a mood of self-improvement a friend asks you to describe the one or two ways by which you think he or she could behave better. You're willing to do so, but need to express yourself in a clear and helpful way. (3, 5, 9)

_____   5. A close companion says that you've been behaving "differently" lately and asks if you know what he or she means. (5, 6, 7)

_____   6. You've grown to appreciate a new friend a great deal lately, and you realize that you ought to share your feelings. (4)

_____   7. An amateur writer you know has just shown you his or her latest batch of poems and asked your opinion of them. You don't think they are very good. It's time for your reply. (5, 9)

_____   8. You've found certain behaviors of an important person in your life have become more and more bothersome to you. It's getting harder to keep your feelings to yourself. (4, 9)

_____ 9. You're invited to a party at which everyone except the host will be a stranger to you. Upon hearing about this, a friend says, "Gee, if I were going I'd feel like an outsider. They probably won't have much to do with you." How do you feel? (2)

_____ 10. A friend comes to you feeling very upset about a recent incident and asks for advice. You suspect that there is more to the problem than just this one incident. You really want to help the friend. (7)

_____ 11. You find yourself defending the behavior of a friend against the criticisms of a third person. The critic accuses you of seeing only what you want to see and ignoring the rest. (2, 4, 5, 9)

_____ 12. A boss or instructor asks you to explain a recent assignment to a companion who has been absent. You are cautioned to explain the work clearly so there will be no misunderstandings. (5)

_____ 13. You ask an acquaintance for help with a problem. She says yes, but the way the message is expressed leaves you thinking she'd rather not. You do need the help, but only if it's sincerely offered. (3, 6, 9)

_____ 14. A roommate always seems to be too busy to do the dishes when it's his or her turn, and you've wound up doing them most of the time. You resent the unequal sharing of responsibility and want to do something about it. (10)

_____ 15. A new acquaintance has become quite interested in getting to know you better, but you feel no interest yourself. You've heard that this person is extremely sensitive and insecure. (1, 2)

You can use the results of this survey in two ways. By looking at each question you can see how satisfied you are with your behavior in that specific type of situation. A response of 1 or 2 on any single question is an obvious signal that you can profit from working on that situation. Parenthetical numbers following each item indicate the chapters of *Looking Out/Looking In* which focus on that subject.

By totaling your score for all of the items you can get an idea of how satisfied you are with your overall ability to communicate in interpersonal situations. A score of 68–75 suggests high satisfaction, 58–67 indicates moderate satisfaction, while 45–57 shows that you feel dissatisfied with your communication behavior nearly half the time.

Another valuable way to use this activity is to make a second inventory at the end of the course. Have you improved? Are there still areas you will need to work on?

1.2 EXPANDING YOUR COMMUNICATION EFFECTIVENESS

◆ **Activity Type: Invitation to Insight**

Purposes

1. To broaden your repertoire of effective communication behaviors and your skill at performing them.
2. To identify the most appropriate communication behaviors in important situations.

Instructions

1. Use the space below to identify two areas in which you would like to communicate more effectively. (e.g., I can't take "no" well. I have trouble telling people what I don't like. People take my intentions wrong.)
2. For each area, identify a person you have observed who communicates in a way that you think would improve your effectiveness. Describe this person's communication behavior.
3. Describe how you could adapt these behaviors to your own life. See page 000 in the text for help.

Example

a. Area in which you would like to communicate more effectively
   Making conversation with people I've just met.
b. Model who communicates effectively in this area   *My friend Rich*
c. Model's behavior   *He asks sincere questions of people he's just met, compliments them enthusiastically, and smiles a lot.*
d. How could you apply these behaviors?   *I can spend more time thinking about people I've just met and less time thinking self-consciously about my own nervousness. Then I can focus on parts of these new people that interest me and let the other person know I'm interested. The key seems to be sincerity: I have to really mean what I say and not use questions and compliments as tricks.*

Situation 1

a. Area in which you would like to communicate more effectively

   _____

b. Model who communicates effectively in this area _____

c. Model's behavior _____

   _____

d. How could you apply these behaviors? _____

   _____

   _____

Situation 2

a. Area in which you would like to communicate more effectively

    _____

b. Model who communicates effectively in this area _____

c. Model's behavior _____

    _____

d. How could you apply these behaviors? _____

    _____

    _____

    _____

Situation 3

a. Area in which you would like to communicate more effectively

    _____

b. Model who communicates effectively in this area _____

c. Model's behavior _____

    _____

d. How could you apply these behaviors? _____

    _____

    _____

    _____

1.3 RECOGNIZING RELATIONAL MESSAGES

◆❖ Activity Type: Skill Builder

Purposes

1. To illustrate that virtually every message has content and relational dimensions.
2. To give you practice recognizing the relational dimension of common messages.
3. To demonstrate that relational messages are ambiguous and need to be verified by perception-checking statements.

Instructions

1. Read the following short article about the content and feeling in messages. http://www.coping.org/communi/model.htm.
2. Read each message below. Picture in your mind the nonverbal behaviors that accompany each of the statements.
3. Describe the relational issues that seem to be involved in each of the situations. Use your text to *label and explain* the relational dimensions of **affinity, immediacy, respect and control** shown by the speaker in each example.
4. In numbers 16-18, record the content of messages you have sent and identify the relational levels involved.

MESSAGE CONTENT	RELATIONAL DIMENSION (AFFINITY, IMMEDIACY, RESPECT, CONTROL)
Example: You tell your romantic partner, " . . . Anyhow, that's what I think. What do you think?"	*Immediacy: I show interest by my tone.* *Affinity: I show liking by my eyes and touch.*
Example: Your instructor invites the class to, "Tell me what's working and what isn't."	*Control: Invites influence over how the course is run.* *Respect: Values the opinions of students.*
1. You ask a friend to come over and the reply is, "I'm sorry, but I have to work."	
2. Someone you live with complains, "You don't help out enough around the house."	
3. Your roommate says, "You're no fun. I think I'm going to bed."	
4. Your boss asks, "Are your hours working out?"	
5. Your boss says, "You'll need a doctor's note to verify your illness."	

6. Your friend teases, "You can't seem to remember the important stuff."	
7. Your parent says, "I know you'll make the right decision."	
8. Your romantic partner says, "I need you to let me know where you are."	
9. Someone reminds you, "Drive carefully."	
10. A family member says you should spend more time at home and you reply, "I'll do what I please."	
11. The doctor's receptionist says, "Can you hold, please?" when you call to make an appointment.	
12. You are getting ready to leave and your partner says, "You're going to wear *that*?"	
13. A friend says, "Fine" and hangs up the phone.	
14. When you ask if you can take time off, your boss rolls eyes and sighs, "Again?"	
15. You tell your friend you don't feel well, and the response is, "Had too good a time last night?"	
Now, record the **content** of messages you've sent (in this column) and identify the **relational dimensions** of those messages in the column to the right.	
16.	
17.	
18.	

1.4 MEDIATED MESSAGES – CHANNELS

❖ **Activity Type: Group Discussion**

Purpose

To evaluate the face-to-face and mediated channels you use to communicate interpersonally.

Instructions

Discuss each of the questions below in your group. Prepare written answers for your instructor, or be prepared to contribute to a large group discussion, comparing your experiences with those of others in your class.

1.   List all the mediated channels you use in addition to face-to-face communication to
     communicate interpersonally.

     _____

     _____

2.   Describe the reasons you use mediated channels. Consider both *practical* reasons (e.g., to
     communicate over distance) and *strategic* ones (e.g., to avoid face-to-face confrontation).

     _____

     _____

3.   Describe situations in which you communicate more effectively using mediated channels.

     _____

     _____

4.   Read the following article about forming relationships online:
     http://www.ascusc.org/jcmc/vol1/issue4/parks.html. Describe how mediated forms of
     communication alter beginning relationships.

     _____

     _____

1.5 YOUR CALL – COMMUNICATION BASICS

◆❖ Activity Type: Skill Builder/Group Discussion

Purposes

1. To reflect upon and judge a communication transaction in terms of the needs of the persons involved.
2. To highlight communication principles and misconceptions that may be present.
3. To use the communication model to identify potential communication problems and recommend solutions.

Instructions

Use the case below and the discussion questions that follow to discuss the variety of communication issues involved in effective communication. Make notes on this page, add other pages on your own, or prepare a group report/analysis based on your discussion. Add your own experiences to individualize the analysis to make it **Your Call**.

Case

Lucia and Caleb have been dating one another exclusively for four months. They both have part-time jobs and hope to complete their college studies within two years. Caleb thinks they should move in together. Lucia is reluctant to agree until she has more commitment from Caleb. Caleb doesn't want to make promises he can't keep. Lucia thinks that if they just communicate more they will be able to solve the problem, but Caleb thinks that talking about it more won't help.

1.   What needs (physical, identity, social, and/or practical) do Lucia and Caleb have?

_____

_____

2.   Identify one element of the communication model that might help explain some of the communication problems they are having and help them communicate more effectively.

_____

_____

3.   What communication principles and/or misconceptions described in Chapter 1 may be operating in this situation?

_____

_____

4.   Describe how Caleb and Lucia could examine the relational dimensions of their messages (affinity, immediacy, respect, and control) to help resolve the problem.

_____

Chapter One

1.6 DEAR PROFESSOR – RELATIONAL RESPONSES

◆❖ Activity Type: Invitation to Insight/Group Discussion

Purposes

1. To examine communication challenges addressed by this chapter.
2. To demonstrate your ability to analyze communication challenges using the concepts in this chapter.

Instructions

1. Read the Dear Professor letter and response below.
2. Discuss Prof Mary's response. Would you add anything or give a different response?
3. Read the second letter. Construct an answer to it, <u>using terms and concepts from this chapter.</u> <u>Underline or boldface the terms and concepts you apply here.</u>
4. If class structure permits, share your answers with other members of the class.

Part A - The letter

Dear Professor,

I've got a problem with my girlfriend. I love her and all, but she's really needy. She wants to be with me all the time, which is nice, but I've got other things in my life to do, like school, work, and being with my friends. I finally went out with some of my friends last night (without her), and she called me five times on my cell phone to say she loved me and see how I was doing. My friends started teasing me, and it was embarrassing. I don't want to leave her but I need a little space. What should I do?   **Brandon**

The response

Dear Brandon,

*Just like all interpersonal relationships, the one that you share with your girlfriend is **unique**. Over time, the two of you have developed social **rules** that are unique to your relationship and guide your interaction. One of these seems to be that you should spend as much time as possible exclusively with each other. While that may have seemed wonderful to you at the beginning of your relationship (and so you cooperated with that emerging rule), you now realize that you want to spend at least some of that time with others and not exclusively with her. As you say, it is not that you don't love her, but you have many **needs** in your life.*

*Since you want to stay in this relationship, I think it is time to **metacommunicate** – talk to her about how you both communicate with other, and what needs each of you has. You'll have to meet her needs, too, of course, so you should approach her with the positive aspects of your relationship first. Tell her how much you appreciate her love, and reaffirm your love for her, looking her in the eyes, smiling, and using a calm and loving tone of voice. (This communicates **affinity and immediacy**.) Explain how you want to be with her a lot of the time, but that when you <u>have</u> to go to work or school, or <u>want</u> to go out with friends without her, that it does not mean you don't love her or respect her. In fact, it means that you are so comfortable with her that you feel secure in your relationship.*

*Tell your girlfriend that you want to share **control** with her in the relationship. She should feel free to make some choices for her time that don't involve you (and you hope she will feel secure in your love, even though you are apart at times). Tell her that you think this will make the choices that you both make about the time you <u>will</u> spend together even more fun. If you want to, suggest that you each check with the other before committing to times apart that don't involve school or work.*

*See how your girlfriend responds up to this point. If she has some **needs** of which you were unaware, you may find you have to adjust your behavior or expectations a bit. If you get no cooperation from her in resolving this issue, you may have to try to take more control in the relationship, telling her that you think you need some relaxation time with former friends, and that you will call her before you go out with them, and after you return home (this avoids you having to tell her, "Don't call me."). If she persists, turn off your cell phone for a few hours.*

A First Look at Interpersonal Relationships

*Hopefully, you both will **metacommunicate** and send the **relational message**s that will keep your relationship happy.*

In hopes for your relational satisfaction,   ***ProfMary***

Part B - The letter

Dear Professor,

My twin brother is in the Army and stationed in Germany. He's coming home in a few months to get married to a woman we all know and like. He has only 2 weeks leave. They don't have very much money so they are planning a very small wedding (immediate family and 2 attendants). The problem is that we have many mutual friends who are not invited because the wedding is so small, and they are all coming to me or calling me, asking me why they aren't invited. I feel bad having to deal with all these friends here who feel slighted. What should I do? ***Jamie***

Your response

Dear Jamie,

_____

_____

_____

_____

_____

_____

_____

_____

_____

_____

_____

_____

Study Guide

CHECK YOUR UNDERSTANDING

Crossword Puzzle

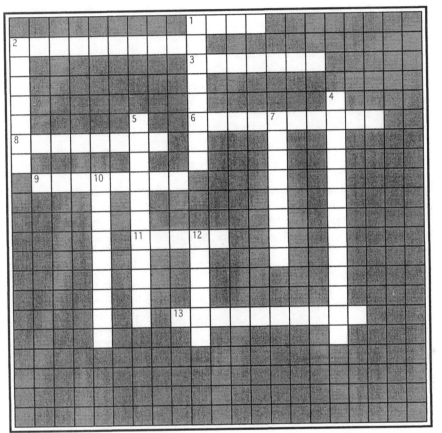

Across
1. two individuals communicating
2. the communication ability to accomplish one's relationship on terms that are acceptable to all parties
3. the social need to influence others
6. behavior that treats others as objects rather than individuals
8. the process of putting thoughts into symbols, most commonly words
9. the degree to which people like or appreciate one another
11. any force that interferes with effective communication
13. the dimension of a message that makes statements about how the parties feel toward one another

Down
1. the process during which a receiver attached meaning to a message
2. the medium through which a messages passes from sender to receiver
4. communication in which the parties consider one another as unique individuals rather than objects
5. the field of experiences that leads a person to make sense of another's behavior
7. one who notices and attends to a message
10. the degree of interest and attention that we feel toward and communicate to others
12. the creator of a message

True/False

Mark the statements below as true or false. Correct false statements on the lines below to create a true statement.

_____ 1. Studies show your physical health may be affected by communication.

_____

_____

_____

_____ 2. The only we learn who we are is through communication, seeing how others react to us.

_____

_____

_____

_____ 3. Communication skills are not more important as a factor helping you get a job than technical competence, work experience, or a degree.

_____

_____

_____

_____ 4. Instrumental goals are the same thing as social needs.

_____

_____

_____

_____ 5. Psychologist Abraham Maslow claims that basic needs must be satisfied before people concern themselves with higher order needs.

_____

_____

_____

_____ 6. The linear view of communication suggests that communication flows in one direction, from sender to receiver.

_____

_____

_____

_____ 7. The transactional model of communication shows that communication is something we do *to* others.

_____

_____

_____

_____ 8. We can decide not to communicate in many ways, such as leaving the room.

_____

_____

_____

_____ 9. Luckily, communication will always help us solve our problems.

_____

_____

_____

_____ 10. Dyadic communication is the earliest form of interaction we experience and the most common type of communication.

_____

_____

_____

_____ 11. What qualifies as competent behavior in one culture might be completely inept, or even offensive, in another.

_____

_____

_____

_____ 12. In order to build a competent relationship, we need to get rid of our need to maintain some space between ourselves and the other person.

_____

_____

_____

_____ 13. You can build competent relationships only if you put the other person's needs ahead of yours.

_____

_____

_____

_____ 14. Effective communicators are able to choose their actions from a wide range of behaviors.

_____

_____

_____

_____ 15. Just knowing about communication skills makes you a better communicator.

_____

_____

_____

Completion

Fill in the blanks below with the correct terms chosen from the list below.

instrumental goals	social needs	identity needs	physiological noise
psychological noise	self-monitoring	control	commitment
cognitive complexity	empathy		

1. _____ are the needs we have to define who we are.

2. _____ are the needs we have to link ourselves with others.

3. _____ are the needs we have to get others to behave in ways we want.

4. _____ refers to the forces within a communicator that interfere with the ability to express or understand a message accurately.

5. _____ refers to the biological factors in the receiver or sender that interfere with accurate reception of messages.

6. _____ is the degree to which the parties in a relationship have the power to influence one another.

7. _____ is the desire to interact and continue the relationship.

8. _____ is the ability to construct a variety of different frameworks for viewing an issue.

9. _____ is the process of paying close attention to your behavior in order to shape the way you behave.

10. _____ is the ability to imagine how an issue might look from the other's point of view.

Multiple Choice

Choose the letter of the communication process element that is most illustrated by the description found below. Italicized words provide clues.

a. encode
b. decode
c. channel
d. message/feedback
e. noise (external, physiological or psychological)
f. environment

_____ 1. The children make a *videotape* of themselves to send to their grandparents instead of writing a *letter*.

_____ 2. Marjorie tries to decide the best way to tell Martin that she can't go to Hawaii with him.

_____ 3. Martin decides Marjorie means she doesn't love him when she says she can't go to Hawaii.

_____ 4. It's so hot in the room that Brad has a hard time concentrating on what his partner is telling him.

_____ 5. Linda *smiles* while Larry is talking to her.

_____ 6. Brooke is daydreaming about her date while Allison is talking to her.

_____ 7. Since Jacob has never been married, it's difficult for him to understand why his married friend Brent wants to spend less time with him.

_____ 8. Whitney says, *"I'm positive about my vote."*

_____ 9. Richard *thinks* Jon wants to leave when he waves to him.

_____ 10. Laura *winks* when she *says* she's serious and *gestures* with her arms.

_____ 11. Erin is from a wealthy family and Kate from a poor one. They have a serious conflict about how to budget their money.

_____ 12. Jack has been feeling a cold coming on all day while he has sat through the meeting.

_____ 13. Levi constructs the best arguments to convince his parents to buy him a new car.

_____ 14. Jessica decides that she will lie to her group members about the reason she missed the meeting last night rather than tell the truth.

_____ 15. "I refuse to go," said Jeremy.

Choose the *best* answer for each of the questions below:

16. According to the quantitative definition of interpersonal communication, interpersonal communication occurs when
    a. two people interact with one another, usually face to face.
    b. you watch a TV show about relationships.
    c. you read a romance novel.
    d. your romantic partner leaves a message on your answering machine.

17. All of the following statements are true <u>except</u>

    a. Communication can be intentional.
    b. Communication is irreversible.
    c. Communication can be unintentional.
    d. Communication is repeatable.

18. All of the following statements are true <u>except</u>

    a. Meanings are not in words.
    b. More communication is not always better.
    c. Communication can solve all your problems.
    d. Communication is not a natural ability.

19. The verbal messages people exchange about their relationship are termed

    a. affinity.
    b. metacommunication.
    c. complementary symmetry.
    d. communication competence.

20. When you are able to perform communication skills without thinking about how you should behave, you have entered the skill stage of

    a. awareness.
    b. awkwardness.
    c. skillfulness.
    d. integration.

CHAPTER 1 STUDY GUIDE ANSWERS

Crossword Puzzle

							¹d	y	a	d			
²c	o	m	p	e	t	e	n	c	e				
h						³c	o	n	t	r	o	l	
a						o					⁴i	
n				⁵e		⁶i	m	p	e	⁷r	s	o	n	a	l
⁸e	n	c	o	d	i	n	g	n		e		t
l		⁹a	f	f	¹⁰i	n	i	t	y	c		e
		m		r				e		i		r
		m		o				v		p	
		e	¹¹n	o	i	¹²s	e		e		e
		d	m			e		r		r
		i	e			n				s
		a	n			d				o
		c	t	¹³r	e	l	a	t	i	o	n	a	l
		y		r						l

True/False

1. T	4. F	7. F	10. T	13. F
2. T	5. T	8. F	11. T	14. T
3. F	6. T	9. F	12. F	15. F

Completion

1. identity needs
2. social needs
3. instrumental goals
4. psychological noise
5. physiological noise
6. control
7. commitment
8. cognitive complexity
9. self-monitoring
10. empathy

Multiple Choice

1. c	5. d	9. b	13. a	17. d
2. a	6. e	10. c	14. a	18. c
3. b	7. f	11. f	15. d	19. b
4. e	8. d	12. e	16. a	20. d

Chapter One

CHAPTER TWO

COMMUNICATION AND IDENTITY: THE SELF AND MESSAGES

OUTLINE

Use this outline to take notes as you read the chapter in the text and/or as your instructor lectures in class.

I. **COMMUNICATION AND THE SELF-CONCEPT**
   A. **Definitions**
      1. Self-concept: The relatively stable set of perceptions you hold of yourself
      2. Self-esteem: Evaluation of your self-worth
   B. **Biological and Social Roots of the Self**
      1. Biology and the self
         a. Personality – characteristic ways of thinking and behaving
         b. Traits – a matter of degree
      2. Socialization and the self-concept
         a. Reflected appraisal (through significant others)
         b. Social comparison (through reference groups)
   C. **Characteristics of the Self-Concept**
      1. The self-concept is subjective
         a. Obsolete information
         b. Distorted feedback
         c. Emphasis on perfection
         d. Social expectations
      2. The self-concept resists change
         a. Failure to acknowledge change
         b. Self-delusion and lack of growth
         c. Defensiveness
   D. **Influences on Identity**
      1. Culture
         a. Individualistic
         b. Collectivistic
      2. Ethnicity
      3. Sex and gender

   E. **The Self-Fulfilling Prophecy and Communication**
      1. Definition: expectations held that make an outcome more likely
      2. Types
         a. Self-imposed
         b. Imposed by others
      3. Influence
         a. Improve relationships
         b. Damage relationships
   F. **Changing Your Self-Concept**
      1. Have a realistic perception of yourself
      2. Have realistic expectations
      3. Have the will to change
      4. Have the skill to change

II. **PRESENTING THE SELF: COMMUNICATION AS IMPRESSION MANAGEMENT**
   A. **Public and Private Selves**
      1. Perceived self
      2. Presenting self (face)
   B. **Characteristics of Identity Management**
      1. We strive to construct multiple identities.
      2. Identity management is collaborative.
      3. Identity management can be deliberate or unconscious.
      4. People differ in their degree of identity management.
   C. **Why Manage Impressions?**
      1. To start and manage relationships
      2. To gain compliance of others
      3. To save others' face

D. How Do We Manage Impressions?
1. Face-to-face impression management
   a. Manner
      1) Words
      2) Nonverbal behavior
   b. Appearance
   c. Setting
2. Impression management in mediated communication

E. Impression Management and Honesty

KEY TERMS

cognitive conservatism
face
identity management
perceived self
personality
presenting self
reflected appraisal

self-concept
self-esteem
self-fulfilling prophecy
significant others
social comparison
reference groups

ACTIVITIES

2.1 WHO DO YOU THINK YOU ARE?

◆ **Activity Type: Invitation to Insight**

Purpose

To identify the biological and social aspects of your self-concept.

Instructions

1. For each category below, supply the words or phrases that describe you best.
2. After filling in the spaces within each category, organize your responses so that the most fundamental characteristic is listed first, with the rest of the items following in order of descending importance.
3. Before you complete the categories below, take an online typology test (The Jung Typology Test); you can score yourself online: http://www.humanmetrics.com/cgi-win/JTypes2.asp . This will get you thinking about the way you describe yourself.

Part A: Identify the elements of your self-concept

1. What cultural or ethnic descriptors are important to describe you (American, Hispanic, Jewish, etc.)?

   a. _____ b. _____ c. _____

2. How would you describe your personality traits (neurotic, stable, extraverted, introverted, etc.)?

   a. _____ b. _____ c. _____

3. What gender or sexual-orientation words describe you (female, gay, heterosexual, etc.)?

   a. _____ b. _____ c. _____

4. How would you describe your social behaviors (friendly, shy, aloof, talkative, etc.)?

   a. _____ b. _____ c. _____

5. What moods or feelings best characterize you (cheerful, considerate, optimistic, etc.)?

   a. _____ b. _____ c. _____

6. How would you describe your physical condition and/or your appearance (fit, sedentary, tall, attractive, etc.)?

   a. _____ b. _____ c. _____

7. What talents do you possess or lack (good artist, lousy carpenter, competent swimmer, etc.)?

   a. _____ b. _____ c. _____

8. How would you describe your intellectual capacity (curious, poor reader, good mathematician, etc.)?

   a. _____ b. _____ c. _____

9. What beliefs do you hold strongly (vegetarian, Christian, passivist, etc.)?

a. _____ b. _____ c. _____

10. What social roles are the most important in your life (brother, student, friend, bank teller, club president, etc.)?

a. _____ b. _____ c. _____

Part B: Arrange your self-concept elements in order of importance

1. _____   16. _____
2. _____   17. _____
3. _____   18. _____
4. _____   19. _____
5. _____   20. _____
6. _____   21. _____
7. _____   22. _____
8. _____   23. _____
9. _____   24. _____
10. _____   25. _____
11. _____   26. _____
12. _____   27. _____
13. _____   28. _____
14. _____   29. _____
15. _____   30. _____

NOTE: You will use these descriptors in Activity 2.2 on the next page.

2.2 SELF-CONCEPT INVENTORY

◆ Activity Type: Invitation to Insight

Purpose

1. To give you a clearer picture of how you see yourself (your perceived self).
2. To illustrate how others perceive you (presenting selves).

Note: Refer to Table 2-4 in your text for a list of self-selected adjectives that describe the perceived and presenting selves of college students.

Instructions

1. Transfer the list of 30 elements of your self-concept from 2.1 to index cards (or strips of paper). If you didn't do 2.1, go back and complete that now.
2. Arrange your cards in a stack, with the one that *best* describes you at the top and the one that *least* describes you at the bottom.
3. Using the Perceived Self column (Table 1), record the order in which you arranged the cards (1 is the most like you). You may leave out some cards or add on to your list.
4. Cover your Perceived Self column and ask two other people (a friend, co-worker, roommate, family member, classmate) to arrange the descriptors in an order in which they see you. Record these perceptions in Tables 2 and 3, being sure to cover your own Table 1 and the Table 2 or 3 that the other person has worked on (so no one sees what the other has written). Record the name/relationship of your evaluator at the top of the appropriate column.
5. Compare the three tables, circling any descriptors that differ from column to column.
6. Answer the questions at the end of this exercise.

Table 1 Perceived Self	Table 2 Presenting Self to	Table 3 Presenting Self to
	_____ (relationship to you)	_____ (relationship to you)
1. _____	1. _____	1. _____
2. _____	2. _____	2. _____
3. _____	3. _____	3. _____
4. _____	4. _____	4. _____
5. _____	5. _____	5. _____
6. _____	6. _____	6. _____
7. _____	7. _____	7. _____
8. _____	8. _____	8. _____
9. _____	9. _____	9. _____
10. _____	10. _____	10. _____

11. _____   11. _____   11. _____

12. _____   12. _____   12. _____

13. _____   13. _____   13. _____

14. _____   14. _____   14. _____

15. _____   15. _____   15. _____

16. _____   16. _____   16. _____

17. _____   17. _____   17. _____

18. _____   18. _____   18. _____

19. _____   19. _____   19. _____

20. _____   20. _____   20. _____

21. _____   21. _____   21. _____

22. _____   22. _____   22. _____

23. _____   23. _____   23. _____

24. _____   24. _____   24. _____

25. _____   25. _____   25. _____

26. _____   26. _____   26. _____

27. _____   27. _____   27. _____

28. _____   28. _____   28. _____

29. _____   29. _____   29. _____

30. _____   30. _____   30. _____

Describe any factors that have contributed in a positive or negative way to the formation of your perceived self (obsolete information, social expectations, perfectionistic beliefs). Include any other factors involved in the formation of your perceived self (for example, certain significant others, any strong reference groups).

_____

_____

_____

_____

Describe any differences between your perceived self and the ways your evaluators perceived you (your presenting selves). What factors contribute to the differences in perception? Whose view is the most accurate and why?

_____

_____

_____

_____

_____

Why might your partners in this exercise view you differently from the way you perceive yourself? Would other people in your life view you like either of the people in this exercise? Give some specific examples with reasons why they would or would not have a similar perception.

_____

_____

_____

_____

_____

Chapter Two

2.3 EGO BOOSTERS AND BUSTERS

◆ Activity Type: Invitation to Insight

Purposes

1. To identify how significant others have shaped your self-concept.
2. To realize how you shape the self-concept of others.

Instructions

1. In the appropriate spaces below describe the actions of several "ego boosters": significant others who shaped your self-concept in a positive way. Also describe the behavior of "ego busters" who contributed to a more negative self-concept.
2. Next, recall several incidents in which you behaved as an ego booster or buster to others. Not all ego boosters and busters are obvious. Include in your description several incidents in which the messages were subtle or nonverbal.
3. Summarize the lessons you have learned from this experience by answering the questions at the end of this exercise.

Ego booster messages you have received

Example

I perceive(d) _my communication lab partner_ **(significant other)** as telling me I am/was ___attractive___

(self-concept element) when he or she kept _sneaking glances at me and smiling during our taping project._

1. I perceived _____ (significant other) as telling me I am/was

    _____ (self-concept element) when he/she _____

    _____

    _____

2. I perceived _____ (significant other) as telling me I am/was

    _____ (self-concept element) when he/she _____

    _____

    _____

Ego buster messages you have received

Example

I perceive(d) _my neighbor_ (significant other) as telling me I am/was _not an important friend_ (self-concept element) when he/she *had a big party last weekend and didn't invite me.*

1. I perceived _____ (significant other) as telling me I am/was

   _____(self-concept element) when he/she _____

   _____

   _____

2. I perceived _____ (significant other) as telling me I am/was

   _____(self-concept element) when he/she _____

   _____

   _____

Ego booster messages you have sent

Example

I was a booster to_my instructor_ when I _told her I enjoyed last Tuesday's lecture._

1. I was a booster to _____ when I _____

   _____

   _____

2. I was a booster to _____ when I _____

   _____

   _____

Ego buster messages you have sent

Example

I was a buster to _my sister_ when I _forgot to phone her or send even a card on her birthday._

1. I was a buster to _____ when I _____

   _____

2. I was a buster to _____ when I _____

_____

_____

Conclusions (Use an additional sheet of paper if necessary)

Who are the people who have most influenced your self-concept in the past? What messages did each one send to influence you so strongly?

_____

_____

_____

_____

What people are the greatest influences on your self-concept now? Is each person a positive or a negative influence? What messages does each one send to influence your self-concept?

_____

_____

_____

_____

Who are the people whom *you* have influenced most greatly? What messages have you sent to each one about his or her self-concept? How have you sent these messages?

_____

_____

_____

What ego booster or buster messages do you want to send to the important people in your life? How can you send each one?

_____

_____

_____

　　　　　Chapter Two

2.4 REEVALUATING YOUR "CAN'TS"

◆ **Activity Type: Invitation to Insight**

Purpose

To identify and eliminate self-fulfilling prophecies which hamper effective communication.

Instructions

1. Complete the following lists by describing communication-related difficulties you have in the following areas.
2. After filling in each blank space, follow the starred instructions that follow the list (*).

Difficulties You Have Communicating with Family Members

Examples

I can't *discuss politics with my dad without having an argument*   because *he's so set in his ways.*
I can't *tell my brother how much I love him*   because *I'll feel foolish.*

1. I can't _____

   because _____

2. I can't _____

   because _____

* Corrections (see instructions at end of exercise)

_____

Difficulties You Have Communicating with People at School or at Work

Examples

I can't *say "no" when my boss asks me to work overtime*   because *he'll fire me.*
I can't *participate in class discussions even when I know the answers or have a question* because *I just freeze up.*

1. I can't _____

   because _____

2. I can't _____

   because _____

* Corrections (see instructions at end of exercise)

_____

_____

Difficulties You Have Communicating with Strangers

Examples

I can't *start a conversation with someone I've never met before*
     because *I'll look stupid.*
I can't *ask smokers to move or stop smoking*
     because *they'll get mad.*

  1. I can't _____

      because _____

  2. I can't _____

      because _____

* Corrections (see instructions at end of exercise)

_____

_____

Difficulties You have Communicating with Friends

Examples

I can't *find the courage to ask my friend to repay the money he owes me*
     because *I'm afraid he'll question our friendship.*
I can't *say no when friends ask me to do favors and I'm busy*
     because *I'm afraid they'll think I'm not their friend.*

  1. I can't _____

      because _____

  2. I can't _____

      because _____

* Corrections (see instructions at end of exercise)

_____

_____

Difficulties You Have Communicating with your romantic partner (Past of present)

Examples

I can't *tell Bill to wear a tie to the party*
     because *he'll laugh at me.*
I can't *bring up going to visit my parents*
     because *we'll fight.*

  1. I can't _____

because _____

2. I can't _____

because _____

* Corrections (see instructions at end of exercise)

_____

Predictions made by others

Examples

You'll never amount to anything.   You can't expect much with your background.
You're just like your father.   The James children never were too bright.

1. _____

2. _____

* Corrections (see instructions at end of exercise)

_____

*After you have completed the list, continue as follows:
  a. Read the list you have made. Actually say each item to yourself and note your feelings.
  b. Now read the list again, but with a slight difference. For each "can't," substitute the word "won't." For instance, "I can't say no to friends' requests" becomes "I won't say no." Circle any statements that are actually "won'ts."
  c. Read the list for a third time. For this repetition substitute "I don't know how" for your original "can't." Instead of saying "I can't approach strangers," say, "I don't know how to approach strangers." *Correct* your original list to show which statements are truly "don't know how's."
  d. For the "Predictions made by others," substitute your strength(s) which makes the prediction untrue (example: "I am my father's child, but I can choose not to repeat behaviors he has that I don't like.").

After completing this exercise, you should be more aware of the power that negative self-fulfilling prophecies have on your self-concept and thus on your communication behavior. Imagine how differently you would behave if you eliminated any incorrect uses of the word "can't" from your thinking.

2.5 SUCCESS IN MANAGING IMPRESSIONS

❖ Activity Type: Skill Builder

Purposes

1. To acknowledge at least one successful aspect of self that you have revealed to others and one that you might improve upon.
2. To reflect on your level of self-monitoring in that instance.

Instructions

1. In groups (or before class written below), describe to one another one instance in which each of you has successfully presented yourself to another person. Describe how you managed that impression of yourself. It may be a significant impression (you got a job you wanted or a date you wanted) or it may be an ongoing, slowly made success (you were a better parent this week or you kept your cool with your roommate during last week's conflict). Describe how you managed manner, setting and/or appearance to create the impression you wanted.
2. Describe to others how aware you were of your own behaviors. Describe whether you had high or low self-monitoring, and how effective or ineffective your level of monitoring was for the impression management situation.
3. Now repeat the process with a less successful self you presented. Again describe manner, setting, appearance and level of self-monitoring. With this face, describe how you might be more successful in identity management.

A. The successful self I revealed to others

_____

_____

_____

How I managed the impression:

Manner _____

_____

Setting _____

_____

Appearance_____

_____

Effectiveness of self-monitoring (level of awareness)

_____

_____

B. The less successful self I revealed to others

_____

_____

_____

How I managed the impression:

Manner _____

_____

Setting _____

_____

Appearance_____

_____

Effectiveness of self-monitoring (level of awareness)

_____

_____

_____

How I might have improved on this identity management:

_____

_____

_____

2.6 MEDIATED MESSAGES – IDENTITY MANAGEMENT

❖ Activity Type: Group Discussion

Purpose

To analyze your presentation of self in mediated communication. Note: Mediated communication involves any extension of our communication abilities (ex: writing, using the telephone or computer).

Instructions

Discuss each of the questions below in your group. Prepare written answers for your instructor, or be prepared to contribute to a large group discussion, comparing your experiences with those of others in your class.

1. Describe ways in which messages from the mass media (i.e., music, television, film, magazines, books) have contributed to your self-concept or the self-concepts of people you know well.

   _____

   _____

2. Your text states that people often prefer mediated channels when their self-presentation is threatened (e.g., have to deliver bad news, want to lie). Give examples to support this claim.

   _____

   _____

3. Identity management is important in mediated contexts. Describe how you manage identity in any mediated contexts you use (written notes, email, instant messaging, personal ad in a newspaper or on a web page).

   _____

   _____

4. Visit www.personals-search.com and read what advice is given for creating an ad. Evaluate this advice based on what you read in this chapter. Would you go out on a date with someone you met through an online dating service? Explain.

   _____

   _____

2.7 YOUR CALL – IDENTITY MANAGEMENT

❖ Activity Type: Group Discussion

Purposes

1. To reflect upon and judge the presentation of self in a communication situation.
2. To highlight self-fulfilling prophecies that may help or hinder a communication transaction.

Instructions

Use the case below and the discussion questions that follow to discuss the variety of communication issues involved in effective communication. Make notes on this page, add other pages on your own, or prepare a group report/analysis based on your discussion. Add your own experiences to individualize the analysis to make it **Your Call.**

Case

Hiroshi was hired in an entry-level position one month ago at a brokerage firm. He wants to succeed at this firm, but is worried that he won't be able fit in with most of the others who have Ivy League degrees and Fifth Avenue wardrobes. Hiroshi's boss graduated from a state college, though, and is very successful at this firm. One of Hiroshi's fellow-workers has just invited him to join a few people from work at a bar on Friday evening.

1. If Hiroshi joins the group at the bar, how should he manage manner, setting and appearance to make the impression he wants?

_____

_____

_____

2. Explain how Hiroshi's social comparison may hinder his self-esteem.

_____

_____

_____

3. What self-fulfilling prophecies might affect Hiroshi's success in this situation?

_____

_____

_____

4. How would you recommend Hiroshi manage his identity at work to present himself effectively.

_____

_____

_____

5. Read *Worst impressions* by Paul McLaughlin on InfoTrac. What advice would you give Hiroshi after reading this article?

_____

_____

_____

2.8 DEAR PROFESSOR – RELATIONAL RESPONSES
◆❖ Activity Type: Invitation to Insight/Group Discussion

Purposes
1. To examine communication challenges addressed by this chapter.
2. To demonstrate your ability to analyze communication challenges using the concepts in this chapter.

Instructions
1. Read the Dear Professor letter and response below.
2. Discuss ProfMary's response. Would you add anything or give a different response?
3. Read the second letter. Construct an answer to it, <u>using terms and concepts from this chapter.</u> <u>Underline or boldface the terms and concepts you apply here.</u>
4. If class structure permits, share your answers with other members of the class.

Part A - The letter

Dear Professor,
I've been in a romantic relationship with Josh for two years, but I don't think it's going anywhere. I want to break it off, but I don't want to hurt Josh. Also, our families and friends all treat us like a couple and act as if they expect us to announce our engagement any day. I'm worried that everyone will say terrible things about me if I'm the one to call it off. **Janessa**

The response

Dear Janessa,
Ethically speaking, you are kind to worry about the effect on Josh after so much time together. Nonetheless, the longer you wait to address the situation, the harder it will become.
*First of all, tell Josh how you feel. Secondly, realize that your **identity** has been tied to Josh for so long that you need to assess your individual strengths and focus on your individual abilities. Finally, avoid the **self-fulfilling prophecy** that terrible things will be said about you; present the good sides of both Josh and yourself to friends and family when you tell them of your (hopefully) mutual decision. You don't need their **approval** for such an individual decision and you can handle a few negative comments if they come your way.*

In hopes for your relational satisfaction,   *ProfMary*

Part B - The letter

Dear Professor,
I met Ben through work and married him 3 years ago. We have a new baby, and now Ben wants me to stay at home with the baby until she's five and goes to kindergarten. I love our baby, but I've never seen myself as only a wife and mother. What should I do? **Robin**

Your response

Dear Robin,

_____

_____

_____

_____

_____

_____

_____

_____

_____

_____

_____

Study Guide

Crossword Puzzle

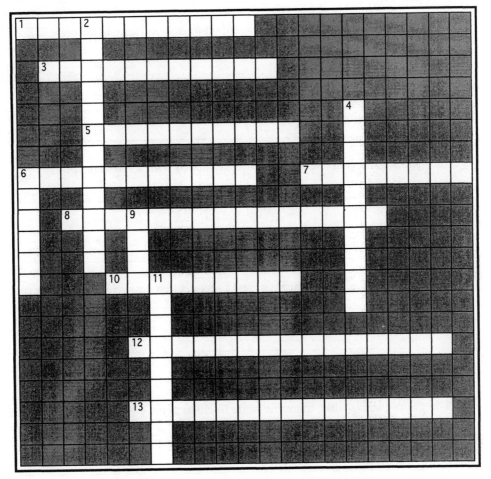

ACROSS

1. characteristic ways that you think and behave across a variety of situations
3. the part of the self-concept that involves evaluations of self-worth
5. a self-concept that is highly dependent on belonging to a group, common in cultures where the main desire is to build connections between the self and others
6. other whose opinion is important enough to affect one's self-concept strongly
7. information about past successes or failures that no longer hold true the image a person presents to others
8. the process of observing one's behavior and using these observations to shape the way one behaves
10. the self whom we believe ourselves to be in moments of candor
12. a prophecy about an event that makes the outcome more likely to occur than would otherwise have been the case
13. a self-concept that is strong "I" oriented, common in cultures where the main desire is to promote the self

DOWN

2. the relatively stable set of perceptions that each individual holds of himself or herself
4. the self a person shows to others
6. comparison of oneself to others
9. another name for the presenting self
11. groups against which we compare ourselves, thereby influencing our self-concept and self-esteem

True/False

Mark the statements below as true or false. Correct statements that are false on the lines below to create a true statement.

_____ 1. Collaboration in identity management means working to agreement about each person's role.

_____

_____

_____

_____ 2. Most researchers agree that we are not born with a self-concept.

_____

_____

_____

_____ 3. The influence of significant others becomes less powerful as we grow older.

_____

_____

_____

_____ 4. People who dislike themselves are likely to believe that others won't like them either.

_____

_____

_____

_____ 5. Research has shown that people with high self-esteem seek out partners who view them unfavorably because they are strong enough to take the criticism.

_____

_____

_____

_____ 6. Luckily, your self-concept is not affected by the language that you speak.

_____

_____

_____

_____ 7. In individualistic societies, there is a higher degree of communication apprehension.

_____

_____

_____

_____ 8. The self-concept is such a powerful force on the personality that it not only determines how you see yourself in the present but also can actually influence your future behavior and that of others.

_____

_____

_____

_____ 9. Research shows that people who believe they are incompetent are more likely than others to pursue rewarding relationships in an attempt to ally themselves with competent people.

_____

_____

_____

_____ 10. The communication strategies we use to influence how others view us are all conscious behaviors.

_____

_____ 11. Every aspect of your self-concept is equally important.

_____

Completion

Fill in the blanks below with the correct terms chosen from the list below.

distorted feedback   obsolete information   self-delusion
ego booster   ego buster   realistic expectations
realistic perceptions   manner   setting
appearance

1. _____ is someone who helps enhance your self-esteem by acting in ways that make you feel accepted, important and loved.

2. _____ is someone who acts to reduce your self-esteem.

3. _____ are messages that others send to you that are unrealistically positive or negative.

4. _____ consists of a communicator's words and nonverbal actions that help create an impression.

5. _____ is information that was once true about you that is no longer true.

6. _____ are the personal items people use to shape an image.

7. _____ is the inability to see a real need for change in the self due to holding an unrealistically favorable picture of yourself.

8. _____ are reasonable goals to set for self-growth.

9. _____ refers to the physical items we use to influence how others view us.

10. _____ are relatively accurate views of the strengths and weaknesses of the self.

Multiple Choice

Identify which principle influences the self-concept in each example. Place the letter of the correct term on the line adjacent to each description.

a. obsolete information
b. distorted feedback
c. emphasis on perfection
d. social expectations

_____ 1. You always scored more points than anyone else on your team in high school. You still think you're the best even though your college teammates are scoring more than you.

_____ 2. You keep getting down on yourself because you can't cook as well as Megan, even though you are a great student and a fair athlete.

_____ 3. You tell everyone how you "blew" the chemistry test and got a "C–" but you don't ever acknowledge your "A's" in math.

_____ 4. Your parents tell you, their friends, and all your relatives about all your wonderful accomplishments, even though you have only average achievement.

_____ 5. Janee says that you are insensitive to her perspective despite your many attempts to listen honestly to her and empathize.

_____ 6. You pay a lot of attention to the magazines showing perfectly dressed and groomed individuals and keep wishing you could look as good as they do.

_____ 7. You think of yourself as the shy fifth grader despite being at the social hub of at least three clubs on campus.

_____ 8. You feel uncomfortable accepting the compliments your friends honestly give you.

_____ 9. You're exhausted by trying to get all A's, work 30 hours a week, and be a loving romantic partner at the same time. You don't see how so many other people manage to get it all done.

_____ 10. "You're the perfect weight," your father tells you despite your recent gain of twenty pounds over the normal weight for your height.

Choose the *best* answer for each statement below:

11. Deciding which part of your self-concept to reveal to others is termed

    a. frontwork.
    b. impression management.
    c. hypocrisy.
    d. two-faced syndrome.

12. The most significant part of a person's self-concept

    a. is the social roles the person plays.
    b. is his or her appearance.
    c. is his or her accomplishments.
    d. will vary from person to person.

13. A sense of identity begins

    a. at conception.
    b. in the womb.
    c. during the first year of life.
    d. at the onset of puberty.

14. Which of the following could be an example of a self-fulfilling prophecy?

    a. Sid is born with a very large nose.
    b. Marguerita has a very large, extended family.
    c. Serge is a Russian immigrant.
    d. Joy has given up on trying to talk to her unreasonable father.

15. The fact that none of us can see ourselves completely accurately illustrates the _____ nature of the self-concept.

    a. subjective
    b. objective
    c. unrealistic
    d. verification

16. Personality traits

    a. are a matter of degree
    b. are an either-or matter
    c. determine all of our communication-related behavior
    d. tend to change more as we grow older

17. The influence of significant others

    a. is the biggest determinant of our self-concept
    b. becomes less powerful as people grow older
    c. is synonymous with the term reflected appraisal
    d. only occurs in people with poor self-concepts

18. Computer-mediated communication

    a. makes it impossible to manage identity
    b. has only disadvantages for impression management
    c. can be an effective tool for impression management
    d. enables the unethical presentation of self

Class________________ Name ______________________________________

CHAPTER 2 STUDY GUIDE ANSWERS

Crossword Puzzle

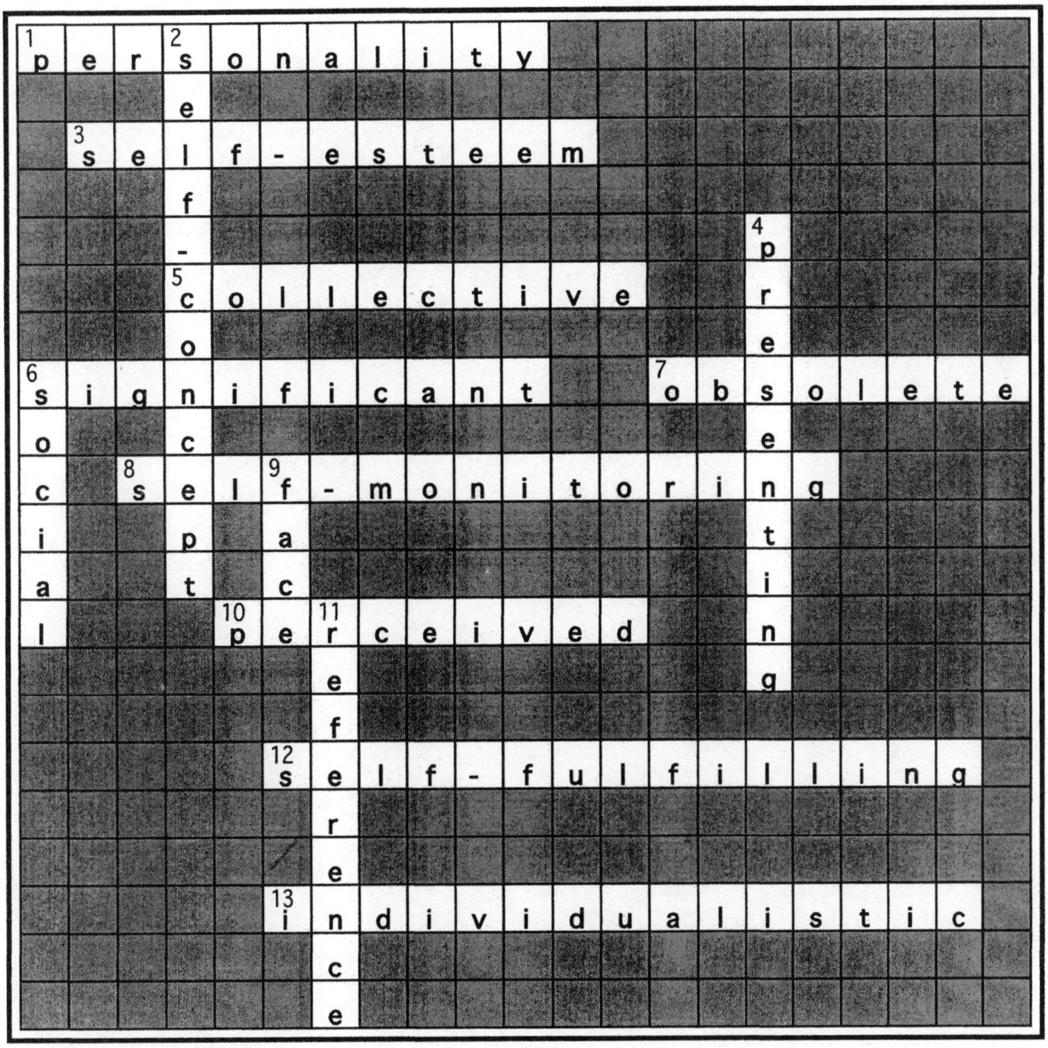
1 personality
2 self-concept
3 self-esteem
4 presenting
5 collective
6 significant
6 social
7 obsolete
8 self-monitoring
9 face
10 perceived
11 reference
12 self-fulfilling
13 individualistic

True/False

1. F	5. F	9. F
2. T	6. F	10. F
3. T	7. F	11. F
4. T	8. T	

Completion

1. ego booster
2. ego buster
3. distorted feedback
4. manner
5. obsolete information
6. appearance
7. self-delusion
8. realistic expectations
9. setting
10. realistic perceptions

Multiple Choice

1. a
2. c
3. d
4. b
5. b
6. c
7. a
8. d
9. c
10. b
11. b
12. d
13. c
14. d
15. a
16. a
17. b
18. c

CHAPTER THREE

PERCEPTION: WHAT YOU SEE IS WHAT YOU GET

OUTLINE

Use this outline to take notes as you read the chapter in the text and/or as your instructor lectures in class.

I. **THE PERCEPTION PROCESS**
   A. **Selection**
      1. Factors that influence selection
         a. Intense stimuli
         b. Repetitious stimuli
         c. Contrast or change in stimulation
         d. Motives
      2. Distortions in selection
         a. Omission
         b. Oversimplification
   B. **Organization**
      1. Figure–ground organization
      2. Perceptual schema
         a. Appearance
         b. Social roles
         c. Interaction style
         d. Psychological traits
         e. Membership
      3. Stereotyping
      4. Punctuation
   C. **Interpretation**
      1. Degree of involvement with the other person
      2. Past experience
      3. Assumptions about human behavior
      4. Attitudes
      5. Expectations
      6. Knowledge
      7. Self-concept
      8. Relational satisfaction
   D. **Negotiation**

II. **INFLUENCES ON PERCEPTION**
   A. **Physiological Influences**
      1. Senses
      2. Age
      3. Health
      4. Fatigue
      5. Hunger
      6. Biological Cycles
   B. **Cultural Differences**
      1. Language translations
      2. Value of talk
      3. Nonverbal behaviors
      4. Ethnicity
      5. Geography
   C. **Social Roles**
      1. Gender Roles
      2. Occupational Roles
   D. **Self-Concept**
      1. Judgments of others
      2. Judgments of self

III. **THE ACCURACY—AND INACCURACY—OF PERCEPTION**
   A. **We Judge Ourselves More Charitably Than Others**
   B. **We Pay More Attention to Others' Negative Characteristics**
   C. **We Are Influenced by the Obvious**
   D. **We Cling to First Impressions**
   E. **We Tend to Assume Others Are Similar to Us**

IV. **PERCEPTION CHECKING**
   A. **Elements of Perception Checking**
      1. Describe behavior
      2. Interpret behavior two ways
      3. Request clarification
   B. **Perception-Checking Considerations**
      1. Completeness
      2. Nonverbal congruency
      3. Cultural rules
         a. Low-context cultures
         b. High-context cultures

V. EMPATHY AND COMMUNICATION
A. Definition
1. Empathy—ability to re-create another's perspective
   a. Perspective taking
   b. Emotional dimension
   c. Genuine concern
2. Sympathy—compassion for another's predicament from your point of view

B. The Pillow Method—A Tool for Building Empathy
1. Position One: I'm right, you're wrong
2. Position Two: You're right, I'm wrong
3. Position Three: Both right, both wrong
4. Position Four: The issue isn't as important as it seems
5. Conclusion: There is truth in all four perspectives

KEY TERMS

androgynous
attribution
empathy
gender role
halo effect
interpretation
narrative
negotiation
organization
perception checking

pillow method
punctuation
selection
self-serving bias
stereotyping
sympathy

ACTIVITIES

3.1 GUARDING AGAINST PERCEPTUAL ERRORS

◆ **Activity Type: Invitation to Insight**

Purposes

1. To identify potentially distorted opinions you have formed about people.
2. To recognize some perceptual errors that may have contributed to those distorted opinions.

Instructions

1. Identify two people about whom you've formed strong opinions. These opinions can be positive or negative. In either case, describe them.
2. Using the checklist provided, comment on the accuracy or inaccuracy of your perceptions of each person. See Chapter 3 of *Looking Out/Looking In* for a more detailed description of the checklist factors. NOTE: Not every factor may apply to each person.
3. Record your conclusions at the end of the exercise.
4. Compare your examples with those of other classmates.

	EXAMPLE	PERSON A	PERSON B
Identify each person. Describe your opinions.	Joni is my wife's good friend. I don't like her; I think she's boring. Her voice is shrill, and I find her annoying.		
1. We judge ourselves more charitably than others.	When Joni lost her job, I thought it was Joni's fault because she's so annoying. Of course, when I got laid off a few months later, I blamed the economy and mentioned nothing about my performance or personality.		
2. We pay more attention to other's negative characteristics.	Joni is attractive, intelligent, successful, and athletic. I tend to disregard all those positive qualities and focus on her shrill voice.		

3. We are influenced by the obvious.	Because she's my wife's friend, Joni is around a lot, so I probably notice her voice or her calls more than is usual.		
4. We cling to first impressions.	I haven't liked Joni from the beginning. She would call right at our dinner time. Even though she doesn't do this any more, I still remember it and I'm sure it influences my opinion of her.		
5. We tend to assume that others are similar to us.	I just assume that Joni will know when I don't want her around. I assume she'd be interested in things I'm interested in. Perhaps she finds the topics I talk about boring, too.		

Conclusions

Based on the observations above, how accurate or inaccurate are your perceptions of other people?

_____

_____

_____

What might you do in the future to guard against inaccurate perceptions of people?

_____

_____

_____

3.2 EXAMINING YOUR INTERPRETATIONS

◆ Activity Type: Invitation to Insight

Purposes

1. To identify the interpretations you make about others' behavior in your important interpersonal relationships.
2. To recognize perceptual factors influencing those assumptions.
3. To consider the validity of your interpretations.

Introduction

There are many ways to interpret what another person says or does. For example, you may notice that a new classmate is wearing a cross necklace and imagine that she is a religious person, or you might notice that a friend isn't making much eye contact with you and assume that he is not telling you the truth.

We usually assume that our interpretations are accurate. In fact, these assumptions might be incorrect or quite different from how the other person sees himself or herself.

Instructions

1. For the next few days, observe three people and use the spaces below to record your interpretations of each.
2. After completing the information below, share your observations with each person involved and see if your interpretations match the explanations of each subject.

Example

Name _Stan Morris_____ context _Neighbor and friend_____
A. Describe an assumption about this person's thoughts or feelings.
   I've been thinking that Stan is mad at me, probably because I've been asking so many favors of him lately.
B. Describe at least two items of behavior (things the person has said or done) that lead you to believe your assumption about this person's thoughts or feelings is accurate.
   1.   When I asked to borrow his backpacking gear he said yes, but he mentioned several times how much it cost him.
   2.   When I asked him for a ride to school last week when my car was in the shop, he said OK but didn't talk much and drove more quickly than usual.
C. Give at least two reasons why your assumption about this person's thoughts or feelings may *not* be accurate. (You may ask the person you are observing for help.)
   1.   Stan is often moody. Even if he is upset, it may not be because of anything I've said or done.
   2.   I'm often hard on myself, taking the blame for anything that goes wrong. Perhaps I'm doing that here, and Stan doesn't mind doing me the favors.
D. Which of the following factors influenced your perception of this person? Explain how each of these factors affected the accuracy or inaccuracy of your interpretations.

   Physiological influences _____

   _____

   Social roles (gender, occupation) Perhaps my being a woman has something to do with my self-doubt. I often wonder if I'm being too "forward" in asking a man for favors.

   Cultural differences _____

Self-concept I often view myself as less desirable as a friend than other people I know. I think this leads me to interpret others' reactions as confirmations of my worst fears whether or not those fears are valid.

Person 1

Name _____ Context _____

A. Describe an assumption you have made about this person's thoughts or feelings.

_____

_____

B. Describe at least two items of behavior (things the person has said or done) that lead you to believe your assumption about this person's thoughts or feelings is accurate.

1. _____

_____

_____

_____

2. _____

_____

_____

C. Give at least two reasons why your assumption about this person's thoughts or feelings may *not* be accurate. (You may ask the person you are observing for help.)

1. _____

_____

_____

_____

2. _____

_____

_____

D. Which of the following factors influence your perception of this person? Explain how each of these factors affected the accuracy or inaccuracy of your interpretations.

Physiological influences _____

_____

_____

Social roles (gender, occupation)_____

_____

_____

Cultural differences _____

_____

_____

Self-concept _____

_____

_____

Person 2

Name _____ Context _____

A. Describe an assumption you have made about this person's thoughts or feelings.

_____

_____

_____

B. Describe at least two items of behavior (things the person has said or done) that lead you to believe your assumption about this person's thoughts or feelings is accurate.

1. _____

_____

_____

2. _____

_____

_____

C. Give at least two reasons why your assumption about this person's thoughts or feelings may *not* be accurate. (You may ask the person you are observing for help.)

1. _____

_____

_____

_____

2. _____

_____

_____

D. Which of the following factors influenced your perception of this person? Explain how each of these factors affected the accuracy or inaccuracy of your interpretations.

Physiological influences _____

_____

_____

Social roles (gender, occupation) _____

_____

_____

Cultural differences _____

_____

_____

Self-concept _____

_____

_____

Person 3

Name _____ Context _____

A. Describe an assumption you have made about this person's thoughts or feelings.

_____

_____

_____

B. Describe at least two items of behavior (things the person has said or done) that lead you to believe your assumption about this person's thoughts or feelings is accurate.

1. _____

_____

_____

2. _____

_____

_____

C. Give at least two reasons why your assumption about this person's thoughts or feelings may *not* be accurate. (You may ask the person you are observing for help.)

1. _____

_____

_____

2. _____

_____

_____

D. Which of the following factors influenced your perception of this person? Explain how each of these factors affected the accuracy or inaccuracy of your interpretations.

Physiological influences _____

_____

_____

Social roles (gender, occupation) _____

_____

_____

Cultural differences _____

_____

_____

Self-concept _____

_____

_____

3.3 SHIFTING PERSPECTIVES (PILLOW METHOD)

◆ Activity Type: Invitation to Insight

PurposeS

1. To help you understand how others view an interpersonal issue.
2. To help you recognize the merits and drawbacks of each person's perspective.
3. To help you recognize how an interpersonal issue may not be as important as it first seems.

Instructions

1. Select one disagreement or other issue that is now affecting an interpersonal relationship.
2. Record enough background information for an outsider to understand the issue. Who is involved? How long has the disagreement been going on? What are the basic issues involved?
3. Describe the issue from each of the four positions listed below.
4. Record your conclusions at the end of this exercise.

Option

With a partner, role-play your situation orally for the class.

Background Information

_____

_____

_____

_____

_____

_____

Position 1: Explain how you are right and the other person is wrong.

_____

_____

_____

_____

_____

_____

Position 2: Explain how the other person's position is correct, or at least understandable.

_____

_____

_____

_____

_____

_____

Position 3: Show that there are both correct (or understandable) and mistaken (or unreasonable) parts of both positions.

_____

_____

_____

_____

_____

Position 4: Describe at least two ways in which the elements developed in positions 1–3 might affect your relationship. Describe at least one way in which the issue might be seen as *less* important than it was originally and describe at least one way in which the issue might be seen as *more* important than it was originally.

_____

_____

_____

_____

_____

Conclusion

Explain how there is some truth in each of the preceding positions. Also explain how viewing the issue from each of the preceding positions has changed your perception of the issue and how it may change your behavior in the future. Explain how this issue and your understanding of it affect your relationship.

_____

_____

_____

3.4 OBSERVATION AND PERCEPTION

❖ Activity Type: Skill Builder

Purposes

1. To report your observations of another person clearly and accurately.
2. To report at least two interpretations about the meaning of your observations to another person.
3. To discuss and evaluate the various choices you have available to you when dealing with perceptual problems.

Instructions

1. As a group, detail three situations below in which there are potential perceptual problems.
2. Use the form below to record behavior for each relationship listed.
3. For each example of behavior, record two plausible interpretations.
4. Record a request for feedback.
5. With others in the group, rehearse how you could share with the person in question each example of behavior and the possible interpretations you have developed.
6. Evaluate the various other options you have to check out perceptions. Describe the probable outcome of each.

Example

Perceptual problem: *Jill's math professor is really annoying her—calling on her for answers and trying to get her involved more in the class. Jill is uncomfortable about this, but she is afraid that the professor might pay even more attention to her if she brings it up.*
Perception checking statement: *Professor Smith, I'm confused about something.*

Behavior: *I've noticed that you call on me quite often—at least once each class, whether or not I raise my hand.*
Interpretation A: *Sometimes I wonder if you're trying to catch me unprepared.*
Interpretation B: *On the other hand, sometimes I think you're trying to challenge me by forcing me to keep on my toes.*
Request for feedback: *Can you tell me why you call on me so often?*

Perception checking options
1. Jill could do nothing. Perhaps it would be better to wait and see if she has been imagining this by watching a bit more.
2. Jill could start initiating answers herself and see if Professor Smith changes behavior.
3. Jill could just tell the Prof that she doesn't like being called on. This might alienate her in the Prof's eyes, however, and might affect her grade.
4. Jill could just ask if the Prof was trying to embarrass her. We thought the Prof might not know what Jill was referring to, though, if she didn't describe behavior. The Prof probably teaches hundreds of students and might not realize what's going on in Jill's eyes.
5. Jill could do the complete perception checking statement we wrote above. Our group thought this has a good chance for success if the Prof didn't get defensive. If Jill could deliver the statement in a non-defensive tone and then follow it up with how much she likes the class, perhaps the Prof would realize how much Jill is bothered.

Situation one

Perceptual problem: _____

_____

_____

Perception-checking statement: _____

Behavior: _____

Interpretation A: _____

Interpretation B: _____

Request for feedback: _____

Perception-checking options:

_____

_____

_____

_____

Situation Two

Perceptual problem: _____

_____

_____

Perception-checking statement: _____

Behavior: _____

Interpretation A: _____

Interpretation B: _____

Request for feedback: _____

Perception-checking options:

_____

_____

_____

Situation Three

Perceptual problem: _____

_____

_____

Perception-checking statement: _____

   Behavior: _____

   Interpretation A: _____

   Interpretation B: _____

   Request for feedback: _____

Perception-checking options:

_____

_____

_____

3.5 PERCEPTION-CHECKING PRACTICE

❖ **Activity Type: Skill Builder**

Purpose

To create effective perception-checking statements.

Instructions

Option A:

Practice writing perception-checking statements for items 1–10 below.

Option B:

1. Join with a partner to create a dyad. Label one person A and the other B.
2. Both A and B should write perception-checking statements for items 1–10 below.
3. A then delivers items 1–5 to B orally. B should use Evaluation Form 3.7 to rate A's responses for these items.
4. B delivers items 6–10 orally to A. A should use Checklist 3.6 to rate B's responses for these items.

Option C:

Practice items 1–10 below orally with a partner. Deliver your best perception check in class while your instructor evaluates you.

Example

Yesterday your friend Erin laughed at a joke about "dumb blonds." You found it offensive.

Perception-checking statement   *Erin, when Joey cracked the dumb blond joke last night, you laughed. I'm wondering if you disapproved of the joke but laughed just to make Joey feel comfortable, or if you really do agree with the premise of that joke that blonds are not as smart as the rest of the population.*
Can you clarify things for me?

1. Last night you saw a recent date walking on the beach, holding hands with someone. You'd like to date again, but don't want to if a current relationship exists. You get a call from the recent date, asking you to a movie and dinner this weekend.

   _____

   _____

2. Ever since the school year began, your father has called weekly, asking how you are doing. He's just asked again.

   _____

   _____

3. Your friend Carlo was driving you home from a party last night when he began to weave the car between lanes on the highway. You were uncomfortable, but didn't say anything then. Now it is the next morning and Carlo shows up to take you to a class. You have decided to bring up the incident.

_____

_____

_____

4. For the last two weeks, when you are leaving your house, your roommate has asked for a ride somewhere. Your roommate has a car, but you haven't seen it lately. You are in a hurry now, and your roommate has just asked for another ride.

_____

_____

_____

5. You return home at night to find your roommate, Tom, reading on the couch. When you walk into the room and greet Tom, he grunts and turns his face away from you and keeps reading.

_____

_____

_____

6. Last week your instructor, Dr. Green, returned your exam with a low grade and the comment, "This kind of work paints a bleak picture for the future." You have approached Dr. Green to discuss the remark.

_____

_____

_____

7. In one of your regular long distance phone conversations you ask your favorite cousin about his romantic life. He sighs and says, "Oh, it's OK, I guess."

_____

_____

_____

8. Your girl or boyfriend (or spouse) announces that she or he plans to spend next Friday night with friends from work. You usually spend Friday nights alone together.

_____

_____

_____

9. Last week your supervisor at work, Ms. White, gave you a big assignment. Three times since then she has asked you whether you're having any trouble with it.

_____

_____

_____

10. Last weekend your next-door neighbor, Steve, raked a big pile of leaves near your property line, promising to clean them up after work on Monday. It's Wednesday, and the wind is blowing the leaves into your yard.

_____

_____

11. One of your classmates sits by you every day in class and you've done a lot of homework together; he's called you at home a few times a week. He suggests that you meet for dinner this weekend.

_____

_____

12. You've noticed one of your office mates looking over at you a number of times during the past few days. At first she looked away quickly, but now she smiles every time you look up and catch her looking at you. You've been under a lot of pressure at work lately and have been extremely busy. You can't understand why she keeps looking at you. You've decided to ask.

_____

_____

_____

3.6 PERCEPTION CHECKING

❖ Activity Type: Oral Skill

Purpose

To evaluate your skill at using perception-checking statements.

Instructions

1. Identify a situation in your life in which a perception check might be appropriate. Describe the situation to the person who will be evaluating your skill check. Possible topics: controversial issues, things that "bug" you, perceived injustices, personal dilemmas, and misperceptions.
2. Deliver a complete perception check to your evaluator, without using notes, following the criteria listed in Chapter 3 of *Looking Out/Looking In* and outlined in the checklist below.
3. Describe on a separate page
   a.   how well perception checking might (or might not) work in the situation you have chosen. If you do not think a complete perception check is the best approach for this situation, explain why and describe a more promising alternative.
   b.   the degree to which you could (or could not) increase your communicative competence by using perception checks in other situations.

Checklist

_____   Describes background for potential perception-checking situation.

_____   Delivers complete perception check

     _____   Reports at least one behavior that describes what the person has said or done.

     _____   States two interpretations that are distinctly different, equally probable, and are based on the reported behavior.

     _____   Makes a sincere request for feedback clarifying how to interpret the reported behavior.

_____   Verbal and nonverbal behavior

     _____   Reflects sincere desire for clarification of the perception.

     _____   Sounds realistic and consistent with style of the speaker.

     _____   Uses nonthreatening, nondefensive voice and eye contact.

_____   Realistically and clearly assesses how perception checking and other alternatives can be used in everyday life.

     _____   In situation described here.

     _____   In other situations (be specific).

How well might perception-checking work in this situation?

_____

_____

_____

How could you increase your competence by using perception-checking in other situations?

_____

_____

_____

3.7 MEDIATED MESSAGES – PERCEPTION

◆❖ **Activity Type: Group Discussion**

Purpose

To investigate perceptual differences in mediated communication.

Instructions

Discuss each of the questions below in your group. Prepare written answers for your instructor, or be prepared to contribute to a large group discussion, comparing your experiences with those of others in your class.

1. Think of ways in which messages sent through mediated messages may contribute to misperceptions. (Example: *I called my grandmother and she thought my tone of voice sounded like I was irritated with her; she didn't say anything to me at the time, but complained to my mother about me.*)

   _____

   _____

2. How do the influences on perception (physiological or cultural differences, social roles, self-concept) affect these mediated misperceptions? (Example: *Physiological: I was tired when I called my grandmother and I know she has age-related hearing problems*)

   _____

   _____

3. Prepare a perception-checking statement that could be used in a mediated context. Specify the mediated channel and the likelihood of success of the perception-checking attempt. (Example: *"When you said in your last e-mail that you were busy on Saturday, I wondered if you had a previous commitment or if you were irritated with me for some reason I'm not aware of and so don't want to see me. What did you mean?" I think this perception-checking statement gives my partner a way to bring up anything that might be wrong, so it has a good likelihood of success.*)

   _____

   _____

   _____

4. Read *Realty check: Misconceptions about online advertising abound. Tackling the perception vs. reality* by Hillary Rosner on InfoTrac. She says, "The Internet must do for advertisers something completely unique and different from what other media do." Explain what she means how that alters our perceptions of these mediated communication efforts.

   _____

   _____

   _____

3.8 YOUR CALL – PERCEPTION

◆❖ Activity Type: Group Discussion

Purposes

1. To explain perceptual factors that may contribute to misunderstandings.
2. To use perception checking to clarify the situation.

Instructions

Use the following case to explore the variety of communication issues involved in communication and perception.

Case

Jorge is a registered nurse at a facility that cares for about 80 elderly patients. Jorge has been at the facility longer than any of the other nurses and has his choice of schedule; he believes he deserves this because of his service and seniority.   There is now a shortage of nurses. Jorge's supervisor, Marisa, has been trying to hire new nurses, some of whom will only work if they can have Jorge's schedule. Marisa and Jorge are meeting to discuss the situation.

1. What factors are likely to influence the perceptions of Jorge and Marisa?

    _____

    _____

2. Prepare perception-checking statements for Jorge and Marisa to deliver to one another.

    _____

    _____

3. How can Marisa and Jorge communicate competently in order to come to a constructive conclusion

    to this situation?

    _____

    _____

4. Read *Quality interpersonal communication - perception and reality*, by Michael B. Coyle on InfoTrac.

    Give Marisa and Jorge advice based on this reading.

    _____

    _____

Chapter Three

3.9 DEAR PROFESSOR – RELATIONAL RESPONSES

◆◆ **Activity Type:** Invitation to Insight/Group Discussion

Purposes

1. To examine communication challenges addressed by this chapter.
2. To demonstrate your ability to analyze communication challenges using the concepts in this chapter.

Instructions

1. Read the Dear Professor letter and response below.
2. Discuss ProfMary's response. Would you add anything or give a different response?
3. Read the second letter. Construct an answer to it, <u>using terms and concepts from this chapter.</u> <u>Underline or boldface the terms and concepts you apply here.</u>
4. If class structure permits, share your answers with other members of the class.

Part A - The letter

Dear Professor,
I was paired with a very attractive, well-dressed woman in my chemistry lab. My initial pleasure at my good fortune quickly turned to dismay. She often came late to lab, she seemed distracted when she was there, and I found myself doing about 70% of our assignments. I decided that she was just a typical, attractive, rich snob, and I became pretty rude and short with her. Yesterday I found out from another person in the lab that she helps take care of her grandfather with Alzheimer's, and sometimes her relief caretaker doesn't show up on time, so that's probably the reason why she's late (and distracted). Now I feel horrible that I judged her so harshly, and I figure she's upset with me for being so rude. How can I fix this situation? **Wadjy**

The response

Dear Wadjy,
*Avoid **mind reading**. You don't know how she feels about you for certain. You can **check out your perceptions**. "When you were late to our l last two labs, I didn't know if you had something come up or if you expected me to cover for you or what. Am I intruding or do you feel OK telling me what's up?" Something like that should at least get you two talking. If she tells you about her situation with her grandfather, you can express **sympathy**, but you are not doing her a favor by doing her work for her. Focus on her mind and treat her in an equitable manner. She might not realize that she's not doing her 50%, so explain your **perception** of the division of labor and see if hers matches yours. Then you might ask how you can help her do her fair share of the work without you feeling resentful. Keep your voice firm and don't be condescending. This should help soften any perception of your rudeness that she may have had.*

In hopes for your relational satisfaction, **ProfMary**

Part B - The letter

Dear Professor,
I'm a sophomore. Because of financial troubles, I had to move into a shared house with six other people (I have no other options). Three of my roommates are freshmen, and they drink, play their music loud, and generally party until 3 or 4 in the morning. I'm trying to work, get some sleep, and study enough to raise my GPA from a disastrous last semester. I've tried talking to them, telling them my mistakes as a freshman and asking for their empathy for my current situation, but they just laugh and call me a nerd. What can I do? **Arturo**

Your response

Dear Arturo,

Study Guide

CHECK YOUR UNDERSTANDING

Crossword Puzzle

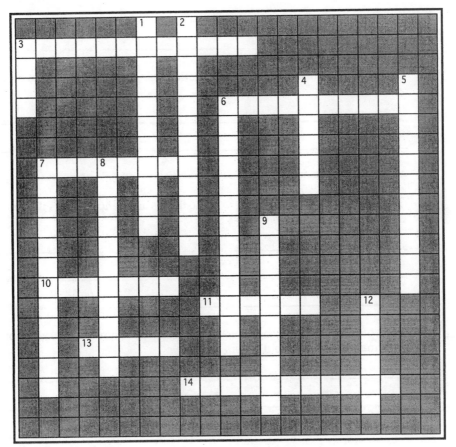

ACROSS

3. a cultural language type valuing social harmony over clarity
6. the process of attaching meaning to our experiences by selecting, organizing and interpreting
7. compassion for another's situation
10. the ability to project oneself into another person's point of view, so as to experience the other's thoughts and feelings
11. cognitive frameworks that allow individuals to organize perceptual data that they have selected from the environment
13. perceptual schema that categorize people according to their social positions
14. the process of attaching meaning to behavior

DOWN

1. a cultural language type using language clearly and logically
2. exaggerated generalizations associated with a categorizing system
3. an effect that illustrates the power of a first impression to influence subsequent perceptions
4. the social and psychological dimensions of masculine and feminine behavior
5. possessing both masculine and feminine traits
7. a bias that illustrates the tendency to interpret and explain information in a way that casts the perceiver in the most favorable manner
8. the process of determining the casual order of events
9. perceptual schema that categorize people according to the groups to which they belong
12. a method that involves an examination of the four sides and middle of a perceptual issue

True/False

Mark the statements below as true or false. Correct statements that are false on the lines below to create a true statement.

_____ 1. Androgynous males have a smaller repertoire of behaviors than masculine males.

_____

_____

_____

_____ 2. Selection, organization, and interpretation comprise the three steps of the perception process.

_____

_____

_____

_____ 3. The fact that we pay attention to some things and ignore others illustrates the fact that selection is an objective process.

_____

_____

_____

_____ 4. Perceptual schema are cognitive frameworks that allow us to classify or organize the information we get about others.

_____

_____

_____

_____ 5. It is wrong to generalize about anybody or any group, even if the generalizations are accurate.

_____

_____

_____

_____ 6. We sometimes view people more favorably if we have a relationship with them.

_____

_____

_____

_____ 7. Adrenal and sex hormones affect the way both men and women relate to each other.

_____

_____

_____

_____ 8. All cultures view talk as desirable, using it for social purposes as well as to perform tasks.

_____

_____

_____

_____ 9. Within the boundaries of a country, most perceptions are similar.

_____

_____

_____

_____ 10. The way we perceive ourselves influences our opinion of self, but not our opinion of others.

_____

_____

_____

_____ 11. Since we are able to perceive with our senses, our perceptions make us aware of all that is going on around us.

_____

_____

_____

_____ 12. People with low self-esteem usually have a high opinion of others.

_____

_____

_____

Completion

Fill in the blanks below with the correct terms chosen from the list below.

narrative	self-serving bias	sympathy
punctuation	perceptual schema	empathy
androgynous	stereotypes	

1. _____ are the cognitive frameworks that allow individuals to organize perceptual data that they have selected from the environment.

2. _____ is the determination of causes and effects in a series of interactions.

3. _____ is a story created by shared perspectives to explain events and behavior.

4. _____ is the tendency to judge ourselves in the most generous terms possible.

5. _____ is the ability to re-create another person's perspective.

6. _____ is feeling compassion for another person's predicament.

7. _____ are exaggerated generalizations associated with a categorizing system.

8. _____ is an example of a psychological sex type that influences perception.

Multiple Choice

RECOGNIZING PERCEPTION-CHECKING ELEMENTS

For each of the following statements, identify which element of the perception-checking statement is missing. Place the letter of the most accurate evaluation of the statement on the line before the statement.

a. This statement doesn't describe behavior.
b. This statement doesn't give two distinctly different interpretations.
c. This statement neglects to request clarification of the perception.
d. There is nothing missing from this perception-checking statement.

_____ 1. "Why did you send me those flowers? Is this a special occasion or what?"

_____ 2. "When you went straight to bed when you came home, I thought you were sick. Are you all right?"

_____ 3. "You must be either really excited about your grades or anxious to talk about something important. What's going on?"

_____ 4. "When you ran out smiling, I figured you were glad to see me and ready to go, or maybe you were having such a good time here you wanted to stay longer."

_____ 5. "I thought you were angry with me when you didn't come over this afternoon like you'd said you would. But then I thought maybe something came up at work. What is it?"

_____   6. "When you told me you expected to get an outline with my report, I thought you were trying to trick me into doing more work, or maybe you didn't realize that wasn't part of my job."

_____   7. "When you told everyone my parents own the company, you must have been indicating I was hired here only because of them. Is that what you think?"

_____   8. "When you passed the ball to me, I thought you wanted me to shoot. Did you?"

_____   9. "Why is it that you're so pleased with yourself? Did you win the lottery or accomplish something great? What's up?"

_____   10. "Dad, when you told my friend Art what a great athlete you think I am, I thought you were either really proud of me and wanted to brag a little, or maybe you wanted to see what Art and I had in common by the way he responded. What were you up to?"

CHAPTER 3 STUDY GUIDE ANSWERS

Crossword Puzzle

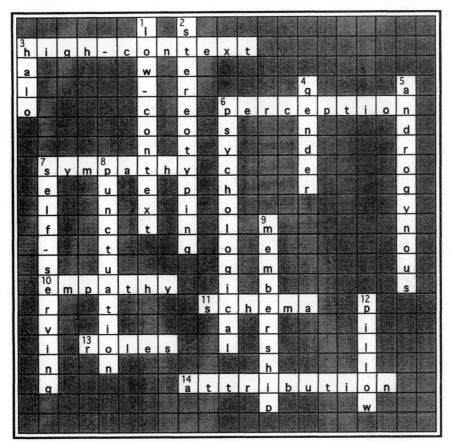

True/False

1. F	4. T	7. T	10. F
2. T	5. F	8. F	11. F
3. F	6. T	9. F	12. F

Completion

1. perceptual schema
2. punctuation
3. narrative
4. self-serving bias
5. empathy
6. sympathy
7. stereotypes
8. androgynous

Multiple Choice

1. b	3. a	5. d	7. b	9. a
2. b	4. c	6. c	8. b	10. d

CHAPTER FOUR

EMOTIONS: THINKING, FEELING, AND COMMUNICATING

OUTLINE

Use this outline to take notes as you read the chapter in the text and/or as your instructor lectures in class.

I. **COMPONENTS OF EMOTIONS**
    A. **Physiological Factors**
    B. **Nonverbal Reactions**
    C. **Cognitive Interpretations**
    D. **Verbal Expression**

II. **TYPES OF EMOTIONS**
    A. **Primary and Mixed Emotions**
    B. **Intense and Mild Emotions**

III. **INFLUENCES ON EMOTIONAL EXPRESSION**
    A. **Personality**
    B. **Culture**
    C. **Gender**
    D. **Social Conventions**
    E. **Fear of Self-Disclosure**
    F. **Social Roles**
    G. **Emotional Contagion**

IV. **GUIDELINES FOR EXPRESSING EMOTIONS**
    A. **Recognize Feelings**
    B. **Expand your Emotional Vocabulary**
    C. **Think about How to Describe Feelings**
        1. Avoid emotional counterfeits
        2. Express verbally
            a. Use single words
            b. Describe what's happening to you
            c. Describe what you'd like to do
        3. Avoid minimizing feelings
        4. Avoid coded feelings
        5. Focus on a specific set of circumstances
    C. **Share Multiple Feelings**

D. **Recognize the Difference between Feeling, Talking and Acting**
E. **Accept Responsibility for your Feelings**
F. **Consider When and Where to Express your Feelings**

V. **MANAGING DIFFICULT EMOTIONS**
    A. **Facilitative and Debilitative Emotions**
        1. Intensity
        2. Duration
    B. **Sources of Debilitative Emotions**
        1. Genetic makeup
        2. The amygdala "fight or flight" response
        3. Thoughts
    C. **Irrational Thinking and Debilitative Emotions**
        1. Fallacy of perfection
        2. Fallacy of approval
        3. Fallacy of shoulds
        4. Fallacy of overgeneralization
            a. Limited amount of evidence
            b. Exaggerated shortcomings
            c. Abuse of the verb "to be"
        5. Fallacy of causation
            a. Believe you cause emotions/pain for others
                1) Fail to have your own needs met
                2) Begin resenting others
                3) Others can't trust you
            b. Believe others cause your emotions
        6. Fallacy of helplessness
        7. Fallacy of catastrophic expectations
    D. **Minimizing Debilitative Emotions**
        1. Monitor your emotional reactions
        2. Note the activating event
        3. Record your self-talk
        4. Dispute your irrational beliefs

KEY TERMS

debilitative emotions
emotional contagion
facilitative emotions
fallacy of approval
fallacy of catastrophic expectations

fallacy of causation
fallacy of helplessness
fallacy of overgeneralization
fallacy of perfection
fallacy of shoulds

mixed emotions
primary emotions
self-talk

ACTIVITIES

4.1 THE COMPONENTS OF EMOTION

❖ **Activity Type: Skill Builder**

Purpose

To identify the components of emotion.

Instructions

1. In groups, read each of the situations described below and describe how the emotions you would experience might manifest themselves in each of the components listed. Compare the responses of group members.
2. After finishing the examples provided for you, record 3 examples of your own (include the incident, the emotion(s), physiological changes, nonverbal reactions, and cognitive interpretations):

Example

Incident: _____

_____

Emotion: _____

Physiological changes: _____

Nonverbal reactions: _____

Cognitive interpretations: _____

1. Incident: Your romantic partner says, "I need to talk to you about something."

   Emotion: _____

   Physiological changes: _____

   Nonverbal reactions: _____

   Cognitive interpretations: _____

2. Incident: You run into an "ex" while out with a new partner.

   Emotion: _____

   Physiological changes: _____

   Nonverbal reactions: _____

   Cognitive interpretations: _____

3. Incident: As you're telling a story, you notice your listener stifle a yawn.

   Emotion: _____

Physiological changes: _____

Nonverbal reactions: _____

Cognitive interpretations: _____

4. Incident: Your professor says, "I'd like to see you in my office after class."

Emotion: _____

Physiological changes: _____

Nonverbal reactions: _____

Cognitive interpretations: _____

Your examples

Incident: _____

_____

Emotion: _____

Physiological changes: _____

Nonverbal reactions: _____

Cognitive interpretations: _____

Incident: _____

_____

Emotion: _____

Physiological changes: _____

Nonverbal reactions: _____

Cognitive interpretations: _____

Incident: _____

_____

_____

Emotion: _____

Physiological changes: _____

Nonverbal reactions: _____

Cognitive interpretations: _____

4.2 FIND THE FEELINGS

❖ Activity Type: Skill Builder

Purposes

1. To distinguish true feeling statements from counterfeit expressions of emotion.
2. To increase your ability to express your feelings clearly.

Instructions

1. In groups, identify the true feeling statements below.
2. Analyze the statements for accuracy of feeling (check your analysis at the end of this exercise).
3. Rewrite statements that do not clearly or accurately express the speaker's feelings. (HINT: Statements that could be prefaced with "I think" are not always expressions of emotions. If the statements could be preceded by "I am," there is a good likelihood that they express feelings.)
4. Record examples of your own at the end of the exercise.

Example

That's the most disgusting thing I've ever heard!
Analysis: *This isn't a satisfactory statement, since the speaker isn't clearly claiming that he or she is disgusted.*
Restatement: *I'm upset and angry that those parents left their young children alone overnight.*

1. You're being awfully sensitive about that.

    Analysis _____

    _____

    Restatement _____

    _____

2. I can't figure out how to approach him.

    Analysis _____

    Restatement _____

    _____

3. I'm confused about what you want from me.

    Analysis _____

    Restatement _____

    _____

    _____

4. I feel as if you're trying to hurt me.

    Analysis _____

    Restatement _____

5. It's hopeless!

   Analysis _____

   Restatement_____

   _____

6. I don't know how to tell you this . . .

   Analysis _____

   Restatement_____

   _____

7. What's bothering you?

   Analysis _____

   Restatement_____

   _____

8. I feel like the rug's been pulled out from under me.

   Analysis _____

   Restatement_____

   _____

9. I feel like I've been stabbed in the back.

   Analysis _____

   Restatement_____

   _____

10. You're so pathetic.

    Analysis _____

    Restatement_____

    _____

Now record three feeling statements of your own. Analyze and, if necessary, restate.

1. _____.

   Analysis _____

   Restatement_____

Class _____   Name _____

_____

2. _____ .

Analysis _____

Restatement _____

_____

3. _____ .

Analysis _____

Restatement _____

_____

Answers to "4.2 Find the Feelings"

1. The speaker here is labeling another's feelings, but saying nothing about his or her own. Is the speaker concerned, irritated, or indifferent to the other person's suspected sensitivity? We don't know. Possible restate: "I worried that I teased you too much about your hair."
2. The emotion here is implied but not stated. The speaker might be frustrated, perplexed, or tired. Possible restate: "I'm unsure about telling him the truth about my absence."
3. Here is a clear statement of the speaker's emotional state. Possible restate: "I'm confused about whether you want me to pay cash or charge it."
4. Just because we say "I feel" doesn't mean a feeling is being expressed. This is an interpretation statement. Possible restate: "I'm anxious about trusting you after you lied to me last week."
5. How does the speaker feel about the hopeless situation: resigned, sad, desperate? We haven't been told. Possible restate: "I feel frustrated after failing three math quizzes in a row.
6. Again, no feeling stated. Is the speaker worried, afraid, distraught? Possible restate: "I'm hesitant to tell you about my plans for summer."
7. This could be a statement of concern, irritation, or genuine confusion. Nonverbal clues can help us decide, but a feeling statement would tell us for certain. Possible restate: "I'm concerned that I may have offended you in some way."
8. Here's a metaphorical statement of feeling, strongly suggesting surprise or shock. This sort of message probably does an adequate job of expressing the emotion here, but it might be too vague for some people to understand. Possible restate: "I feel insecure right now since I didn't get the job I was expecting."
9. This is another metaphorical statement feeling, strongly suggesting hurt or betrayal. While this statement may do an adequate job of expressing the emotion, it might be misinterpreted by some people, and it might be too strong a statement for the actual situation. Possible restate: "I'm hurt that Joe told you what I said in confidence."
10. This is the speaker's interpretation of someone else's behavior. It contains no feeling. Possible restate: "I'm irritated that you say you're tired and overworked when I've just worked a week of 10-hour shifts."

Chapter Four

4.3 STATING EMOTIONS EFFECTIVELY

❖ Activity Type: Skill Builder

Purpose

To help you express the emotions you experience clearly and appropriately.

Instructions

1. Identify what's ineffective or unclear about each of the following feeling statements.
2. Rewrite the feeling statements making them more effective. Use the following guidelines for sharing feelings (see pages 144-149 in your text):
    Recognize feelings
    Describe feelings (concise, not discounted/minimized, not coded, focused on specifics)
    Share multiple feelings
    Differentiate between feeling, talking, and acting
    Accept responsibility for your feelings
    Consider when and where to express

FEELING STATEMENT	IDENTIFY INEFFECTIVE, UNCLEAR ELEMENTS/REWRITE STATEMENT
Example *When you complimented me in front of everyone at the party, I was really embarrassed.*	*I didn't express the mixed emotions I was feeling. I could have expressed this better by saying, "When you complimented me last night at the party, I was glad you were proud of me, but I was embarrassed that so many people heard it."*
1. You should be more sensitive.	
2. When you get all over me, I can't think straight.	
3. You've got some nerve telling me what to do.	
4. Well, I guess you don't really care about this – or me.	
5. When you act like that, I don't want to be seen with you.	

FEELING STATEMENT	IDENTIFY INEFFECTIVE, UNCLEAR ELEMENTS/REWRITE STATEMENT
6. You infuriate me.	
7. Why should I help you now? You never show me any appreciation.	
8. I was a little ticked off when you didn't show up.	
9. You jerk—you forgot to put gas in the car!	
10. It's about time you paid up.	
11. I guess I'm a little attracted to him.	
12. With all that's happened, I feel like I'm in a time warp.	

4.4 SELF-TALK

❖ **Activity Type: Skill Builder**

Purposes

1. To discover the self-talk in many common statements.
2. To identify fallacies in self-talk.
3. To dispute irrational self-talk.

Instructions

1. In groups, analyze the statements below.
2. Expand the self-talk behind each statement by using details from your personal experience to help discover things people think but often do not admit.
3. Identify any fallacies contained in the self-talk: approval, overgeneralization, perfection, helplessness, shoulds, catastrophic expectations, causation
4. Dispute any irrational self-talk.
5. As a group, record the most common examples of your own self-talk, the fallacies involved, and the disputing you need to do to keep emotionally healthy.

STATEMENT	SELF-TALK	FALLACIES	DISPUTE ANY FALLACIES
Example: She's so critical.	She never has anything good to say. She drives me crazy. I can't stand her. I'll never be able to make her happy.	Overgeneralization, Causation, Helplessness, Approval	I need to focus on the good things she does say, not the criticisms. She doesn't make me crazy; I let her get to me. If I don't like what she is saying at the moment, I can leave. It would be nice to please her, but I don't need her approval to be happy.
1. No one appreciates me around here.			
2. He's so moody.			
3. I don't know why I even bother to study for her stupid tests			

STATEMENT	SELF-TALK	FALLACIES	DISPUTE ANY FALLACIES
4. Why can't he be more sensitive to my feelings?			
5. She is so embarrassing because she has no manners.			
6. He's a jerk just like his brother.			
7. She's the perfect woman. I'll be completely happy forever.			
8. I'll never get out of here with all her talking.			
9. I can't believe you told me to buy this worthless car.			
10. It's no use talking to him; he's so unreasonable.			

Class _____   Name _____

YOUR OWN EXAMPLE STATEMENT	SELF-TALK	FALLACIES	DISPUTE ANY FALLACIES
1.			
2.			
3.			
4.			
5.			

Emotions

4.5 DISPUTING IRRATIONAL THOUGHTS

◆ Activity Type: Invitation to Insight

Purpose

To help you minimize debilitative emotions by eliminating irrational thinking.

Instructions

1. Use the chart opposite to record incidents in which you experience communication-related debilitative emotions. The incidents needn't involve overwhelming feelings: mildly debilitative emotions are appropriate for consideration as well.
2. For each incident (activating event), record the self-talk that leads to the emotion you experienced.
3. If the self-talk you've identified is based on any of the irrational fallacies described in *Looking Out/Looking In,* identify them.
4. In each case where irrational thinking exists, dispute the irrational fallacies and provide an alternative, more rational interpretation of the event.
5. After completing the examples, record your conclusions here (or put them on a separate page):

Conclusions

1. What are the situations in which you often experience debilitative emotions?

   _____

   _____

2. What irrational beliefs do you subscribe to most often? Label them and explain.

   _____

   _____

   _____

3. How can you think more rationally to reduce the number and intensity of irrational emotions? (Give specific examples related to other aspects of your life, as well as referring to the activating events you have described in this exercise.)

   _____

   _____

   _____

   _____

ACTIVATING EVENT	SELF-TALK	IRRATIONAL FALLACIES	EMOTION(S)	DISPUTE FALLACIES AND PROVIDE ALTERNATE RATIONAL THINKING
Example: *Getting ready for job interview*	*The employer will ask me questions I can't answer. I'll mess up for sure. I'll never get a good job—it's hopeless!*	*catastrophic failure* *overgeneralization* *helplessness*	*apprehension* *despair*	*I've prepared for the questions and the interview, so if I'm asked something I don't know, I'll say I'll get back to them on that. I have interpersonal skills. I'll find a good job with time and effort.*
1.				
2.				
3.				
4.				
5.				

4.6 MEDIATED MESSAGES – EXPRESSING EMOTION

◆ Activity Type: Group Discussion

Purpose

To evaluate the expression of emotion in mediated contexts.

Instructions

Discuss each of the questions below in your group. Prepare written answers for your instructor, or be prepared to contribute to a large group discussion, comparing your experiences with those of others in your class.

1. Describe how to recognize emotions communicated in mediated channels such as written notes, e-mail, telephone, instant messaging/chat.

_____

_____

2. Emotional expression may be more difficult in a mediated context (e.g., lack of touch or facial expression to communicate your empathy). On the other hand, mediated contexts may make emotional expression easier (e.g., write a note upon the death of someone rather than face them). Cite examples from your life where you used mediated contexts to express emotion.

_____

_____

_____

_____

3. In written communication, some stylistic devices (underlining, exclamation marks, emoticons like the smiley, winking or sad face) indicate emotion. How effective do you think these can be in expressing emotion?

_____

_____

4. Go to the following site: www.eq.org; double click on <u>Virtual EQ</u> and then <u>32 Keys</u>. Read at least three of the collections of ideas about life related to emotions (fear, stress, happiness, despair, etc.). How does reading about these ideas online affect your emotions?

_____

_____

Emotions

4.7 YOUR CALL – EXPRESSING EMOTION

◆ **Activity Type: Group Discussion**

Purpose

To evaluate the expression of emotion in an applied context.

Instructions

Use the case below and the discussion questions that follow to discuss the variety of communication issues involved in effective communication. Make notes on this page, add other pages on your own, or prepare a group report/analysis based on your discussion. Add your own experiences to individualize the analysis to make it *Your* Call.

Case

Marcos and Alessandra have been dating for over a year. They love each other and are considering marriage, but each has at least one big reservation about the other. Marcos thinks Alessandra is moody; it seems that one minute she is "up" and happy with everyone, including him, and the next she is feeling crabby and criticizes everything about him. Alessandra finds Marcos difficult because he seems to keep everything inside; she wants him to tell her when he feels good and bad in detail, but he says nothing or responds with only a few words.

1. What is the appropriate level of emotional expression between dating partners? Do you think either Marcos or Alessandra should change the way they express their emotions?

   _____

   _____

2. Do you think Marcos and Alessandra perceive the emotional climate of the other accurately? Are there any influences on emotional expression that might exist here (culture, gender, social conventions, social roles, emotional contagion, fear of self-disclosure)?

   _____

   _____

3. Can you identify any irrational fallacies (approval, overgeneralization, perfection, helplessness, shoulds, catastrophic expectations, causation) in either Marcos or Alessandra that might trigger debilitative emotions?

   _____

   _____

4. What would you recommend that Marcos and Alessandra do about their emotional expressions?

   _____

   _____

4.8 DEAR PROFESSOR – RELATIONAL RESPONSES

◆❖ **Activity Type:** Invitation to Insight/Group Discussion

Purposes

1. To examine communication challenges addressed by this chapter.
2. To demonstrate your ability to analyze communication challenges using the concepts in this chapter.

Instructions

1. Read the Dear Professor letter and response below.
2. Discuss ProfMary's response. Would you add anything or give a different response?
3. Read the second letter. Construct an answer to it, <u>using terms and concepts from this chapter.</u> <u>Underline or boldface the terms and concepts you apply here.</u>
4. If class structure permits, share your answers with other members of the class.

Part A - The letter

Dear Professor,
My older brother (he's 23) has a job, but really lives off my parents. He doesn't pay rent or for food, and he keeps trying to borrow money. My mother feels sorry for him and gives him money and things that she really can't afford. I've tried to tell him he should be on his own, but he comes back with, "Well, they give you all this money for college." (He never went to college.) How can I help him and the family without alienating him? **Hiro**

The response

Dear Hiro,
It is good that you are concerned about your parents and don't want anyone (even a family member) taking advantage of them.
First of all, remember that your parents are responsible for their own behavior, and they can choose to let your brother live at home, feed him, and give him things if they choose. It's nice that you are concerned about them and want to protect them, but they are capable of resisting your brother's requests.
Secondly, try to identify the **mixed emotions** *you may be experiencing—anger, resentment, jealousy, concern, uncertainty, indignation—and ask yourself whether those* **emotions** *are connected to your brother's behavior, your parents' behaviors, or your own. What are the* **activating events** *that trigger your* **self-talk**? *Do you feel these emotions when you see your brother just hanging around the house, or when he actually asks for something? Do you feel these emotions when your mother says something to or about your brother or when you find out she's given him something?*
Lastly, identify any **irrational thinking** *that may lead to your emotions. Do you think your parents* **shouldn't** *give him money or he* **shouldn't** *ask for it? Do you think that you or your brother* **cause** *financial problems for your parents? Do you think that, because you are in college, you deserve all the financial resources available?*
You probably can't make your brother do (or stop doing) what you want. But you can handle your own emotions toward him and your parents effectively.

In hopes for your relational satisfaction,   ***ProfMary***

Part B - The letter

Individually, or as a group, use the following site to refresh your memory of rational-emotive therapy before you answer the following Dear Professor letter:
http://www.threeminutetherapy.com/rebt.html

Dear Professor,
My roommate is having a problem breaking off from her boyfriend. He's emotionally abusive, and she probably knows (at some level, at least) that she needs to break if off. She seems scared to be alone, so she never quite is able to finalize a break. What should I do to help her? **Ali**

Your response

Dear Ali,

_____

_____

_____

_____

_____

_____

_____

_____

_____

_____

_____

_____

Study Guide

CHECK YOUR UNDERSTANDING

Crossword Puzzle

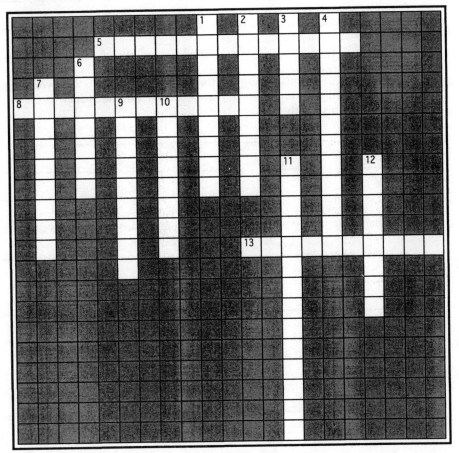

ACROSS

5. changes that are the body's internal physical response to strong emotions
8. emotions that prevent a person from functioning effectively
13. a fallacy of thinking that believes that no errors should be made in communication performance

DOWN

1. interpretation or thought that accompanies strong emotions
2. reactions that are the visible physical signs in response to strong emotions
4. emotions that contribute to effective functioning
6. basic emotions
7. the nonvocal process of thinking
9. the strength of an emotion
10. the fallacy of thinking that believes that acceptance is needed from others
11. stimuli that are sensations activated by movement of internal tissues
12. the length of an emotion

True/False

Mark the statements below as true or false. Correct statements that are false on the lines below to create a true statement.

_____ 1. In a study of 5000 people, people who described themselves as shy behaved differently than those who said they were not shy.

_____

_____

_____

_____ 2. Women consistently score higher than men on the PONS test, which measures the ability to recognize emotions that are expressed in the facial expressions, movements, and vocal cues of others.

_____

_____

_____

_____ 3. People are generally better at recognizing emotions of members of the opposite sex.

_____

_____

_____

_____ 4. In mainstream North American society, the unwritten rules of communication encourage the direct expression of most emotion.

_____

_____

_____

_____ 5. "I feel confined" is an emotional counterfeit statement.

_____

_____

_____

_____ 6. Using many words to express a feeling is better than just summarizing feelings in a few words.

_____

_____

_____

_____ 7. A certain amount of negative emotion can be constructive or facilitative.

_____

_____

_____

_____ 8. Outgoing people report more negative emotions in everyday life than do those who are less social.

_____

_____

_____ 9. Subscribing to the myth of perfection may diminish your own self-esteem, but it won't keep others from liking you.

_____

_____

_____

_____ 10. The rational-emotive approach to emotions is nothing more than trying to talk yourself out of feeling bad.

_____

_____

_____

_____ 11. People from colder climates are more emotionally expressive than those who live in warmer climates.

_____

_____

_____

Completion

Fill in the blanks below with the correct terms chosen from the list below.

catastrophic expectations   helplessness   causation
overgeneralization   shoulds   approval
perfection   activating event   monitoring
disputing

1. _____ is an irrational fallacy that operates on the assumption that if something bad can possibly happen, it will.

2. _____ is an irrational fallacy that suggests that satisfaction in life is determined by forces beyond your control.

3. _____ is an irrational fallacy based on the belief that emotions are the result of other people and things rather than one's own self-talk.

4. _____ is an irrational fallacy that makes a broad claim based on a limited amount of evidence.

5. _____ is an irrational fallacy based on the inability to distinguish between what is and what ought to be.

6. _____ is an irrational fallacy in which people go to incredible lengths to seek acceptance from virtually everyone.

7. _____ is an irrational fallacy in which people believe that worthwhile communicators should be able to handle every situation with complete confidence and skill.

8. _____ is the single large incident or series of small incidents that lead to thoughts or beliefs about the incident.

9. _____ is the process of recognizing the physiological, nonverbal, and cognitive components of emotions.

10. _____ is the process of recognizing mistaken thinking and developing alternative thinking.

Multiple Choice

Choose the letter of the irrational fallacy contained in the self-talk found below.

a. perfection
b. approval
c. shoulds
d. overgeneralization

e. causation
f. helplessness
g. catastrophic expectations

_____ 1. "If only I didn't put my foot in my mouth when I ask someone out."

_____ 2. "I just can't initiate conversations—that's all there is to it."

_____ 3. "He shouldn't be off with his friends on Friday night."

_____ 4. "If she doesn't like this shirt, I'll be so upset."

_____ 5. "There was a major fire the last time we left; there will probably be an earthquake this time."

_____ 6. "He's never romantic."

_____ 7. "She's a cold fish; I'm lucky if I get a kiss."

_____ 8. "You ought to drink less."

_____ 9. "You're going to die going to Mexico at spring break."

_____ 10. "I've had a class in interpersonal communication; I can't believe I insulted her just now."

_____ 11. "Shaw makes me so mad with all his great grades."

_____ 12. "She'll be devastated if I break up with her."

_____ 13. "It's not even worth trying to reach him."

_____ 14. "I hope they don't notice how much weight I've gained."

Choose the best answer for each of the statements below.

15. Which of the following statements about emotions and culture is true?

   a. The same events will generate the same emotions in all cultures.
   b. Certain basic emotions are experienced by all people around the world.
   c. People from different cultures express happiness and sadness with facial difference.
   d. Fear of strangers is as strong in Japan as it is in the U.S.

16. Which of the following statements about gender and emotion is true?

   a. Women and men are equally likely to express feelings of vulnerability.
   b. Men and women are equally good at recognizing the emotions of others.
   c. Men are less bashful about revealing their strengths and positive emotions than women are.
   d. Women are more likely than men to express negative emotions..

17. All of the following statements about social emotion are true *except*:

   a. Genuine emotional expressions are rare.
   b. The emotions that people do share directly are usually positive.
   c. Married couples disclose positive and negative feelings about absent third parties.

d.   Married couples disclose hostility feelings regularly.

18.   Which of the following is a true feeling statement?

    a.   "I feel like watching a movie."
    b.   "I feel like you're lonely."
    c.   "I'm irritated by the ticking clock."
    d.   "I'm totally involved."

19.   Which of the following *best* improves the expression of emotion in the statement "I feel like giving up"?

    a.   "I'm frustrated after asking him to pay his telephone bill three times."
    b.   "I'm going to kill him."
    c.   "I am going to tell the landlord about this frustrating situation."
    d.   "I feel he's been unreasonable."

20.   How could you improve your emotional expression in the statement "She makes me so totally upset, always thinking she is better than everyone else."

    a.   take out the "totally."
    b.   focus on a specific set of circumstances
    c.   accept responsibility for your feelings
    d.   All of the above could improve the statement.
    e.   The statement is fine the way it is.

21.   The biological structure in the brain that scans our experiences for threats is called the:

    a.   sentinel
    b.   neurotransmitter
    c.   amygdala
    d.   proprioceptor

CHAPTER 4 STUDY GUIDE ANSWERS

Crossword Puzzle

```
                 1c    2n    3m    4f
          5 p  h  y  s  i  o  l  o  g  i  c  a  l
       6p                    g     n     x     c
     7s  r                   g     n  v  e        i
  8d  e  b  i  l 9i  t 10a  t  i  v  e        d        l
     l      m      n      p      t     r        i
     f      a      t      p      i     b        t
     -      r      e      r      v     a   11p     a  12d
     t      y      n      o      e     l    r      t   u
     a             s      v             o    i      r
     l             i      a             p    v      a
     k             t      l       13p  e  r  f  e  c  t  i  o  n
                   y      i             i          i
                                        o          o
                                        c          n
                                        e
                                        p
                                        t
                                        i
                                        v
                                        e
```

True/False

1. F	3. F	5. F	7. T	9. F
2. T	4. F	6. F	8. F	10. T
				11. F

Completion

1. catastrophic expectations
2. helplessness
3. causation
4. overgeneralization
5. shoulds
6. approval
7. perfection
8. activating event
9. monitoring
10. disputing

Multiple choice

1. a	5. g	9. g	13. f	17. d
2. f	6. d	10. a	14. b	18. c
3. c	7. d	11. e	15. b	19. a
4. b	8. c	12. e	16. c	20. d
				21. c

Chapter Four

LANGUAGE: BARRIER AND BRIDGE

OUTLINE

Use this outline to take notes as you read the chapter in the text and/or as your instructor lectures in class.

I. **LANGUAGE IS SYMBOLIC**

II. **UNDERSTANDINGS AND MISUNDERSTANDINGS**
 A. **Understanding Words: Semantic Rules**
  1. Equivocation
  2. Relative language
  3. Static evaluation
  4. Abstraction
   a. High abstraction advantages
   b. High abstraction problems
    1) Stereotyping
    2) Confusing others
 B. **Understanding Structure: Syntactic Rules**
 C. **Understanding Context: Pragmatic Rules**

III. **THE IMPACT OF LANGUAGE**
 A. **Naming and Identity**
 B. **Affiliation, Attraction, and Interest**
  1. Convergence
  2. Divergence
  3. Liking/interest
   a. Demonstrative pronoun choice
   b. Sequential placement
   c. Negation
  3. Duration
 C. **Power**
 D. **Disruptive Language**
  1. Fact-opinion confusion
  2. Fact-inference confusion
  3. Emotive language
 E. **The Language of Responsibility**
  1. "It" statements
  2. "But" statements
  3. Questions vs. statements

  4. "I" and "You" language
   a. "I" language
    1) Describes the other's behavior
    2) Describe your interpretation
    3) Describe your feelings
    4) Describe consequences the other person's behavior has for you
   b. Advantages of "I" language
    1) Accepts responsibility
    2) Reduces defensiveness
    3) Is more accurate
   c. Reservations about "I" language
    1) Anger can restrict you
    2) Other can still gets defensive
    3) Can sound artificial
  5. "We" language
    1) Can signal inclusion and commitment
    2) Can speak improperly for others

III. **GENDER AND LANGUAGE**
 A. **Content**
  1. Some common topics
  2. Sex talk restricted to same gender
  3. Many topics vary by gender
 B. **Reasons for Communicating**
  1. Men and women - build and maintain social relationships
   a. Men use more joking and good-natured teasing
   b. Women focus more on feelings, relationships and personal problems
  2. Women—nourish relationships
   a. Support
   b. Equality
   c. Keep conversation going
   d. Express empathy

3. Men - accomplish tasks
   a. Accomplish jobs
   b. Control
   c. Preserve independence
   d. Enhance status

C. Conversational Style
1. Men judge, direct, and make "I" references
2. Women more questions, intensifiers, emotional references, uncertainty and contradictions
3. Accommodation

D. Nongender Variables
1. Occupation
2. Social philosophy
3. Gender

V. LANGUAGE AND CULTURE
A. Verbal Communication Styles
1. Direct/indirect (low-context and high-context cultures)
2. Elaborate/succinct
3. Formality/informality

B. Language and World View
1. Linguistic determinism (Sapir-Whorf hypothesis)
2. Linguistic relativism

KEY TERMS

abstraction ladder
abstract language
behavioral language
"but" statements
convergence
divergence
emotive language
equivocal language
high-context cultures
"I" language
"it" statements
linguistic determinism

linguistic relativism
low-context cultures
powerless speech mannerisms
pragmatic rules
relative words
Sapir-Whorf hypothesis
semantic rules
static evaluation
syntactic rules
"we" language
"you" language

ACTIVITIES

5.1 MISUNDERSTOOD LANGUAGE
❖ Activity Type: Skill Builder

Purpose
To recognize and change language that contributes to misunderstanding.

Instructions
1. In groups, label the language contained in each of the sentences below as relative language, static evaluation, or equivocal language.
2. Rewrite each sentence in more precise language.
3. Write your own examples of each variety of language in the spaces provided.
4. Compare your answers with those of the other groups.

Example 1
I'm trying to diet, so give me a **small piece of cake.**
Language *Relative language*
Revised statement *I'm trying to diet, so give me a piece of cake about half the size of yours.*

Example 2
Helen is a troublemaker.
Language *Static evaluation*
Revised statement *Helen told my mother that I was out until 3 a.m. with Jim.*

Example 3
She's a very **mature** child for her age.
Language *Equivocal language*
Revised statement *Ellen is 5 years old and sat through the concert without wiggling or talking for 2 hours.*

1. I want to talk about **our future.**

   Language _____

   Revised statement _____

   _____

2. They're real **party animals.**

   Language _____

   Revised statement _____

   _____

3. She's very **conservative.**

   Language _____

   Revised statement _____

4. Our candidate is trying to bring about a more **peaceful** world.

   Language _____

   Revised statement _____

5. I haven't done my laundry for **a long time**.

   Language _____

   Revised statement _____

6. Your essay should be **brief**.

   Language _____

   Revised statement _____

7. He's **smart**.

   Language _____

   Revised statement _____

8. My job isn't **taking me anywhere**.

   Language _____

   Revised statement _____

9. Let's take a **break**.

   Language _____

   Revised statement _____

10. She's such a **braggart**.

    Language _____

    Revised statement _____

    _____

11. Stanley is a **righteous** person.

    Language _____

    Revised statement _____

    _____

12. We need to make some **changes** around here.

    Language _____

    Revised statement _____

    _____

13. He's a **bigot**.

    Language _____

    Revised statement _____

    _____

14. Let's take a **break**.

    Language _____

    Revised statement _____

    _____

15. You've got **really poor attendance**.

    Language _____

    Revised statement _____

    _____

16. She is **too tense**.

    Language _____

    Revised statement _____

    _____

Now write your own examples of each type of language and revise the statements to illustrate alternative language.

1. Equivocal language _____

   _____

   Revised _____

   _____

2. Relative language _____

   _____

   Revised _____

   _____

3. Static evaluation _____

   _____

   Revised _____

   _____

5.2 BEHAVIORAL LANGUAGE

❖ Activity Type: Skill Builder

Purpose

To increase the clarity of your language by using behavioral descriptions.

Instructions

In each of the situations below, change the language to describe behavior in specific terms. Remember to focus on the <u>behavior</u> (e.g., Bev <u>did</u> "x," rather than Bev <u>is</u> "x"). If you are giving instructions, be specific enough (low abstractions) to clearly get your idea across to someone else.

Example 1
John's a live wire.
John ran a 5K in the morning, volunteered for two hours at the homeless shelter in the afternoon, and then danced at a party until dawn.

Example 2
Go over that way.
Go across the footbridge, turn right, go up the five large steps to the third building on your left.

1. Jesse can't deal with issues.

   _____

   _____

2. Natalka needs to get real.

   _____

   _____

3. You can't rely on Randy.

   _____

   _____

4. That teacher is a slave-driver.

   _____

   _____

5. Get organized.

   _____

   _____

6. Jill drives me to distraction.

    _____

    _____

7. Josh just blows me off when I have something important to say.

    _____

    _____

8. She acts snippy.

    _____

    _____

9. Jack's motivated.

    _____

    _____

10. My parents are understanding.

    _____

    _____

11. Shelley flakes on me all the time.

    _____

    _____

12. You're too emotional.

    _____

    _____

13. Get something good to watch this time.

    _____

    _____

14. Don't act so needy.

    _____

    _____

5.3 RESPONSIBLE LANGUAGE

◆❖ Activity Type: Skill Builder

Purpose

To rewrite evaluative statements into descriptive ones.

Instructions

1. Rewrite each evaluative "you" language statement into descriptive "I" language.
Use all four elements of the complete "I" statement:
   a. Describe the other person's behavior
   b. Give your interpretation of the behavior
   c. Describe your feelings
   d. Give the consequences that the other person's behavior has for you.

Be careful to
   a. Use specific, low level abstractions
   b. Take responsibility for your thoughts and feelings (don't say, "I feel you're . . .")
   c. Avoid loaded terms like "it seems as if," "you wouldn't <u>even</u>", "you could <u>at least</u>," finally, whenever, ever since, always, "I can't believe that," "Just because," "When you kept on," etc.
2. Record examples of your own at the end and rewrite them.

Example 1

"You don't care about my feelings."
> *Behavior: I saw you in the coffee shop with your old girlfriend when you told me you had to work.*
> *Interpretation: I thought you lied to me about where you were going.*
> *Feeling: I'm hurt and confused.*
> *Consequence: I'm not sure of where we stand in our relationship.*

Example 2

"That was a dumb move!"
> *Behavior: You used the high setting to dry my favorite cotton shirt.*
> *Interpretation: I figured you were in a rush and forgot it needed a lower setting.*
> *Feeling: I'm irritated*
> *Consequence: because it doesn't fit me now.*

1. "You ruined my day."

   Behavior_____

   Interpretation _____

   Feeling _____

   Consequence_____

2. "You're such a drama queen."

   Behavior_____

   Interpretation _____

   Feeling _____

Consequence_____

3. "You clearly can't be trusted."

Behavior_____

Interpretation _____

Feeling _____

Consequence_____

4. "Stop trying to control my life."

Behavior_____

Interpretation _____

Feeling _____

Consequence_____

5. "You don't trust me ever."

Behavior___Always Questioning the decisions/actions

Interpretation _____

Feeling _____

Consequence_____

6. "You're so full of yourself."

Behavior_____

Interpretation _____

Feeling _____

Consequence_____

7. "You make me doubt our relationship."

Behavior_____

Interpretation _____

Feeling _____

Consequence_____

8. "You have a bad attitude."

   Behavior_____

   Interpretation _____

   Feeling _____

   Consequence_____

9. "You weren't there for me."

   Behavior_____

   Interpretation _____

   Feeling _____

   Consequence_____

10. "You're not really trying to get a job."

   Behavior_____

   Interpretation _____

   Feeling _____

   Consequence_____

Record your own "you" language statements here. Rewrite them using "I" language.

11. _____.

   Behavior_____

   Interpretation _____

   Feeling _____

   Consequence_____

12. _____.

   Behavior_____

   Interpretation _____

   Feeling _____

   Consequence_____

5.4 "I" LANGUAGE

❖ Activity Type: Oral Skill

Purpose

To evaluate your skill in delivering "I" language statements.

Instructions

1. Form partners. Identify situations in your lives in which both "you" and "I" language messages might be delivered.
2. Deliver in a realistic manner both a "you" message and an "I" message to your partner according to Chapter 5 of *Looking Out/Looking In* and outlined in the checklist below.
3. Describe on a separate sheet of paper
   a.   how well "I" language might (or might not) work in the situation you have chosen. If you do not think "I" language is the best approach for this situation, explain why and describe a more promising alternative.
   b.   the degree to which you could (or could not) increase your communicative competence by using "I" language in other situations.

Checklist

_____   Delivers a "you" message to partner.

_____   Delivers the same message in "I" language, without using notes

      _____   Describes the other's specific behavior(s) in specific, behavioral terms, using non-evaluative language

      _____   Describes own feelings arising from other's behavior(s).

      _____   Describes consequences of other's behavior(s) as appropriate for self, for the other person, for third parties, or for the relationship.

_____   Verbal and nonverbal behavior

      _____   Reflects responsibility for "owning" the message.

      _____   Sounds realistic and consistent with personal style.

_____   Evaluates probably outcome of "I" message, explaining how it might be used or adapted in this and other real-life situations.

5.5 EFFECTIVE LANGUAGE

◆ **Activity Type: Invitation to Insight**

Purpose

To analyze the types of language you use and the effectiveness of each.

Instructions

1. For each of the situations below, record the type of language used by the speaker. Evaluate its effectiveness. If you cannot identify with the situation, substitute one of your own.
2. Record the language you would use in response. Again, record your own situation and language if you have a relevant one.
3. Label the type of your language and its effectiveness. Focus on high and low abstraction, powerful or powerless speech mannerisms, facts or opinions, inferences, high- and low-context language styles and language and worldview.
4. Describe any alternative language you could use and its relative effectiveness.

Example

Situation: Your supervisor at work has called you aside three times this week to correct work you have done. Each time she says, "You've messed up on this."

Type of language used with you/effectiveness: *My supervisor used "you" language and high abstraction. It wasn't very effective with me because I wasn't sure exactly what I'd messed up on, and I got very defensive, thinking she was about to fire me. She was very direct with me, however; she didn't keep silent about what was bothering her (this is consistent with the low-context culture in which I live).*

Language you'd use in response: *"You're on me all the time about something or other."*

Type of language and effectiveness: *"You" language and high abstraction. This is probably not very effective. My supervisor is likely to get defensive. Actually, my supervisor may think this is "helpful" and "caring" behavior and not realize that I am feeling hassled and threatened.*

Alternative language: *"Ms. Gomez, I'm worried that I'm not doing my job correctly because you've corrected me three times this week." This "I" language is more likely to let Ms. Gomez know what specifically is bothering me without raising a good deal of defensiveness. She's likely to appreciate my directness and specific request for help.*

1. Situation: Your romantic partner has been extremely busy with school and work the last two weeks, and you've been feeling left out. When you suggest going out to a party, your partner replies, "You need a personal circus to have fun."
   Type of language used with you/effectiveness:

   _____

   _____

   Language you'd use in response:

   _____

   _____

   Type of language and effectiveness:

   _____

Alternative language:

_____

_____

2. Situation: You have a hard time saying "no." Lately your roommate has been asking you to do chores that are not your responsibility. Tonight the roommate says, "You're such a great roommate. You won't mind doing the dishes for me tonight since I've got a date and you're just staying home anyway, will you?"

Type of language used with you/effectiveness:

_____

_____

Language you'd use in response:

_____

_____

Type of language and effectiveness:

_____

_____

Alternative language:

_____

_____

3. Situation: Cousins of yours are moving to town. They just called, addressing you by your old family nickname and said, "You lucky person, you get to have the pleasure of our company for a while until we find a place to live."

Type of language used with you/effectiveness:

_____

_____

_____

_____

_____

Language you'd use in response:

_____

_____

Type of language and effectiveness:

_____

_____

Alternative language:

_____

_____

4. Situation: You're working on a project with a partner from class, and the partner says, "We'll never get this done. You're too meticulous about everything."

Type of language used with you/effectiveness:

_____

_____

Language you'd use in response:

_____

_____

Type of language and effectiveness:

_____

_____

_____

Alternative language:

_____

_____

5. Situation: Your boss's five-year-old is visiting the workplace. The child has broken two items and is now running from door to door, laughing loudly. Two customers look your way. Your boss says, "Chip off the old block, huh? Really an energetic kid!"

Type of language used with you/effectiveness:

_____

_____

Language you'd use:

_____

_____

Type of language and effectiveness:

_____

_____

Alternative language:

_____

_____

Record a situation of your own here:

6. Situation:

Type of language used with you/effectiveness:

_____

_____

Language you'd use in response:

_____

_____

Type of language and effectiveness:

_____

_____

Alternative language:

_____

_____

5.6 MEDIATED MESSAGES – LANGUAGE

◆❖ Activity Type: Group Discussion

Purpose

To analyze the use of language in mediated contexts.

Instructions

Discuss each of the questions below in your group. Prepare written answers for your instructor, or be prepared to contribute to a large group discussion, comparing your experiences with those of others in your class.

1. Our identity is tied to the names we use. Discuss how the name(s) you use in mediated contexts make a difference (e.g., *your e-mail address or your chat room identity*).

    _____

    _____

2. The language used in an answering machine or voice mail message can be very businesslike or very informal. Discuss the pros and cons of formal versus informal mediated messages.

    _____

    _____

3. Sometimes people fail to adapt their language style to the medium they are using (e.g., *they leave a 5-minute e-mail or voice mail that should have been summarized in 30 seconds*). Should different mediated channels contain more language or less? Specify two different mediated channels and how much language is appropriate for each.

    _____

    _____

4. Describe the gender or social role differences you have noticed in the <u>language</u> of mediated communication. (Example: *My son seems much more comfortable "talking" about emotions through e-mail, whereas my daughter prefers the telephone.* (Example: *My husband's secretary uses very informal language to address me in an e-mail that she never uses with me face-to-face.*)

    _____

    _____

5. Read the following article about gender differences in email communication: http://iteslj.org/Articles/Rossetti-GenderDif.html. Report on which finding you thought was the most interesting.

    _____

    _____

5.7 YOUR CALL – LANGUAGE

❖ Activity Type: Group Discussion

Purpose

To analyze language choices and their effect on a relationship.

Instructions

Use the case below and the discussion questions that follow to discuss the variety of communication issues involved in effective communication. Make notes on this page, add other pages on your own, or prepare a group report/analysis based on your discussion. Add your own experiences to individualize the analysis to make it **Your Call**.

Case

Professor Segura paired Takako and Magdalena as class project partners. After three weeks both Takako and Magdalena came to see Professor Segura, each complaining about the other. Takako called Magdalena a "flake" and said she didn't work hard enough and didn't take the project seriously. Magdalena said that Takako was "arrogant," wanted the project done only her way, and didn't care about all the commitments Magdalena had. It is too late in the semester for Professor Segura to give them new partners.

1. Notice the language that Takako and Magdalena are using about one another. What effect does using this language have on the successful completion of their project?

   _____

   _____

2. What high level abstractions are Takako and Magdalena using? Write specific language here that could improve their situation.

   _____

   _____

3. Give an example of an "I" language statement that could improve the situation (from Takako, Magdalena, or Professor Segura).

   _____

   _____

4. Gender and culture may influence the way language is used here. Describe differences mentioned in your text and how those differences might apply to this situation.

   _____

   _____

5.8 DEAR PROFESSOR – RELATIONAL RESPONSES

◆❖ Activity Type: Invitation to Insight/Group Discussion

Purposes

1. To examine communication challenges addressed by this chapter.
2. To demonstrate your ability to analyze communication challenges using the concepts in this chapter.

Instructions

1. Read the Dear Professor letter and response below.
2. Discuss ProfMary's response. Would you add anything or give a different response?
3. Read the second letter. Construct an answer to it, <u>using terms and concepts from this chapter.</u> <u>Underline or boldface the terms and concepts you apply here.</u>
4. If class structure permits, share your answers with other members of the class.

Part A - The letter

Dear Professor,
I have an ex-girlfriend that I want out of my life. Steph and I broke up 3 months ago after dating for a year. She still comes over to visit my mother, and she's always calling or hanging out with my friends. I don't want to be perceived as immature about this, but I don't want to be friends; I don't want to see her anymore at all. It is uncomfortable for me, and I want her to go away. How can I make this happen? **Chet**

The response

Dear Chet,
If Steph was with you for a year, she probably became friends with your friends, so it may be unreasonable of you to demand that she stop seeing them because she is no longer dating you. On the other hand, if you believe she is just associating with them with the hope that she will get back with you, you need to make it clear to Steph (and your mother and your friends) that you are finished.

*Avoid **equivocal** language; if you tell others that you and Steph are "just friends," they may think that means you don't mind her being around. Avoid **emotive** language; remember you once thought Steph was friendly and socially at ease when she talked easily with your mother and friends, but now you find that same behavior pushy and inappropriate.*

*Take **responsibility** for your behavior by using **"I" statements**: "Mom, I'm uneasy when Steph drops by to talk with you because we broke up 3 months ago. When I see her talking easily with you in our house every weekend, I think she's trying to get back with me through you. I want to be sure you know how I feel about Steph and why I leave the house whenever she arrives." Or "Heh, guys, I want you to know that I'm not going to be at the party Saturday. Steph said she was going, and I find it really uncomfortable to be around her since we broke up. I just want you guys to know that I want to stay friends with you and that my absence Saturday is about Steph, not you."*

You may find that your mother and your friends will help you work through this adjustment in your relationship with Steph once they clearly understand your situation.

In hopes for your relational satisfaction,   ***ProfMary***

Part B - The letter

Note: Before you answer this letter, read "Words that hurt: What you should never say to your kids: at: http://familyfun.go.com/raisingkids/child/skills/feature/dony108scwords/. Compare the scapegoating, comparing, shaming, negativity, threats and guilt trips to the language mentioned below.

Dear Professor,
    My dad is very concerned about being a nice guy and a good father. When he does something "nice" it is in his definition, not mine. So he takes me to do something and tells me, "Isn't this great?" or "Aren't you lucky to be doing this?" I don't think it's great or that I'm lucky. When I say that, he gets irritated and makes me feel like the bad guy. What should I do? **Darryl**

Your response

Dear Darryl,

©2005 Thomson Learning, Inc.

Study Guide

CHECK YOUR UNDERSTANDING

Crossword Puzzle

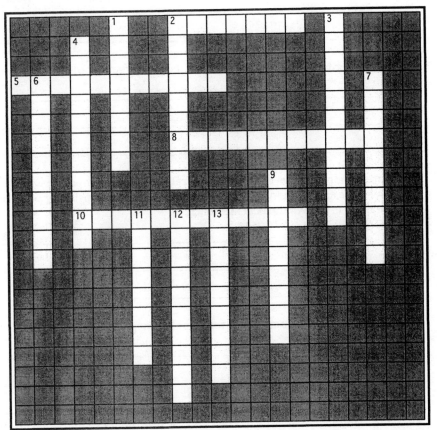

ACROSS

2. language that conveys the sender's attitude rather than simply offering an objective description
5. the use of general terms rather than specific language
8. the process of adapting one's speaking style to match that of others
10. a linguistic device that shows the transitory nature of many objects and behaviors

DOWN

1. language terms that gain their meaning from comparison
2. language that conveys the sender's attitude rather than simply offering an objective description
3. cultures that use language primarily to express thoughts, feelings, and ideas as clearly and logically as possible

4. the linguistic theory that holds that a culture's worldview is unavoidably shaped and reflected by the language its members speak
6. a language account that refers only to observable phenomena
7. speaking in a way that emphasizes differences from others
9. rules of language that govern the ways symbols can be arranged, as opposed to the meanings of those symbols
11. rules that govern what meaning language has, as opposed to what structure it has
12. a moderate linguistic theory that argues that language exerts a strong influence on the perceptions of the people who speak it
13. rules that govern what interpretation of a message is appropriate in a given context

True/False

Mark the statements below as true or false. For statements that are false, correct them on the lines below to create a true statement.

_____ 1. Words are not arbitrary symbols; they have meaning in and of themselves.

_____

_____

_____

_____ 2. According to research, your name is likely to affect people's first impressions of you.

_____

_____

_____

_____ 3. Since research shows that people are rated as more competent when their talk is free of powerless speech mannerisms, it is obvious that a consistently powerful style of speaking is always the best approach.

_____

_____

_____

_____ 4. Ambiguity and vagueness are forms of language that are to be avoided at all costs.

_____

_____

_____

_____ 5. "We" language works well when you include others so that you can speak for them.

_____

_____

_____

_____ 6. "How are we feeling today?" is an example of "we" language.

_____

_____

_____

_____ 7. "Democrats are more responsive to the people than Republicans are" is an example of a fact statement.

Class _____   Name _____

_____

_____

_____

_____ 8. According to research on language and gender, on the average, men discuss with men different topics than women discuss with other women.

_____

_____

_____

_____ 9. Men are more likely to use language to accomplish the job at hand, while women are more likely to use language to nourish relationships.

_____

_____

_____

_____ 10. A person from the United States is more likely to value direct language than is someone from Japan.

_____

_____

_____

Completion

Fill in the blanks below with the correct terms chosen from the list below.

succinctness   equivocation   convergence   divergence   polite forms
tag questions   elaborateness   hedges   disclaimers   subscripting
formality   informality

1. _____ is the process of adapting one's speech style to match that of others with whom the communicator wants to identify.

2. _____ in language use involve denying direct responsibility for the statement, such as "I could be wrong, but . . . "

3. _____ of language involve using respectful terms of address, such as "You're welcome, ma'am."

4. _____ involves speaking in a way that emphasizes a person's differences from the other persons with whom he or she is speaking .

5. _____ in language use involves using words that more than one commonly accepted definition, such as "They eat *healthy* food."

6. _____ in language use involve a negation statement, such as *"Didn't you think that party was boring?"*

7. _____ in language use make less of the feeling or intention statement, such as "I'm *rather* upset."

8. _____ in language use involves dating to reduce static evaluation, such as "Kanako is nervous."

9. _____ involves speaking with few words, and it is usually most extreme in cultures where silence is valued.

10. _____ involves speaking with rich and expressive terms, sometimes involving strong assertions and exaggerations.

11. _____ is a way of using correct grammar as a way of defining social position in some cultures.

12. _____ is a way of using language that is casually friendly and does not reflect a series of relational hierarchies in a particular culture.

Class _____ Name _____

Multiple Choice

Label the examples of language given below by writing the letter of the language type illustrated on the line in front of the example.

a. inference
d. emotive word
b. relative word
e. equivocal language
c. euphemism

_____ 1. John didn't call **so he must be angry**.

_____ 2. I have a **stomach problem**.

_____ 3. That place is **expensive**.

_____ 4. That guy is a real **hunk**.

_____ 5. I'd like **recognition** for my work.

_____ 6. The bathroom **needs some air**.

_____ 7. We need to make **progress** tonight.

_____ 8. The funeral director pointed out the **slumber room**.

_____ 9. He showed up, **so he must agree**.

_____ 10. That's a real **smart trick you pulled**.

_____ 11. My brother is a **sanitation engineer**.

_____ 12. Ian gave a **long** speech.

_____ 13. My grandfather is **young**.

_____ 14. My sister is a **pill**.

Choose the letter of the *least* abstract alternative to the high abstraction terms.

_____ 15. Jo's **constantly complaining**.

    a. Jo whines a lot.
    b. Jo complains often about the workload.
    c. Jo told me three times this week that she feels overworked.
    d. Every time we meet, Jo complains about all the work she does.

_____ 16. He can **never** do **anything** because he's **always busy**.

    a. He couldn't take me to the dinner because he had to work.
    b. He can never do anything fun because he's always working.
    c. He didn't ever take time off to be with me.
    d. He works too much so we have a boring life.

_____ 17. There are **a lot of problems** associated with **freedom**.

    a. Freedom carries with it responsibility.

b. Since I moved into my own apartment, I have to pay ten bills.

c. I don't like all the responsibility of living on my own.

d. My economic responsibilities limit my freedom.

_____ 18. Shannon is **worthless** as a roommate.

a. Shannon is always gone, so she's really not part of our house.

b. Shannon never does her part around here.

c. Shannon's jobs seldom get done around here.

d. Shannon has attended only one of our six house meetings.

_____ 19. Carlos is the **most wonderful friend**.

a. Carlos has never told anyone about my fear of failing.

b. Carlos listens to me about everything.

c. Carlos is the best listener I've ever met.

d. I can trust Carlos implicitly with all my secrets.

_____ 20. Keiko **goes overboard** in trying to make people like her.

a. Keiko gave everyone on the team a valentine.

b. Keiko is the biggest kiss-up you ever met.

c. I think Keiko is trying to make my friends like her better than me.

d. I want Keiko to stop trying to outdo everybody else.

CHAPTER 5 STUDY GUIDE ANSWERS

Crossword Puzzle

The crossword puzzle solution:

Across/Down entries spelled out in grid:
- emotive
- abstraction
- convergence
- subscripting
- low-context
- divergence

Grid letters:
```
              r      e m o t i v e      l
          d   e      q                  o
          e   l      u                  w
5 a b s t r a c t i o n              7 d
    e   e   t      v                 c   i
    h   r   i      o                 o   v
    a   m   v    8 c o n v e r g e n c e
    v   i   e      a              9 s   r
    i   n              l            y   t   g
    o   i                              e   e
    r 10 s u b 11 s 12 c 13 r i p t i n g n
    a   m      e   r   a      t      x   c
    l         m   e   a   g   a         e
              a   l   a   m   c
              n   a   t   a   t
              t   t   i   t   i
              i   i   v   a   c
              v   c   s   t
              c   i      i
                  s      c
                  m
```

True/False

| 1. | F | 3. | F | 5. | F | 7. | F | 9. | T |
| 2. | T | 4. | F | 6. | F | 8. | T | 10. | T |

Completion

1. convergence
2. disclaimers
3. polite forms
4. divergence
5. equivocation
6. tag questions
7. hedges
8. subscripting
9. succinctness
10. elaborateness
11. formality
12. informality

Multiple choice

1.	a	5.	e	9.	a	13.	b	17.	b
2.	c	6.	c	10.	d	14.	d	18.	d
3.	b	7.	e	11.	c	15.	c	19.	a
4.	d	8.	c	12.	b	16.	a	20.	a

Chapter Five

CHAPTER SIX

NONVERBAL COMMUNICATION: MESSAGES BEYOND WORDS

OUTLINE

Use this outline to take notes as you read the chapter in the text and/or as your instructor lectures in class.

I. **NONVERBAL COMMUNICATION**
   A. Importance – emotional impact
   B. Definition: Those Messages Expressed Nonlinguistic Means

II. **CHARACTERISTICS OF NONVERBAL COMMUNICATION**
   A. Nonverbal Skills are Important
   B. All Behavior Has Communicative Value
      1. Deliberate
      2. Unintentional
   C. Nonverbal Communication Is Primarily Relational
      1. Identity management
      2. Definition of relationships we want with others
      3. Conveyance of emotion
   D. Nonverbal Communication Serves Many Functions
      1. Repeating
      2. Substituting
      3. Accenting
      4. Regulating
      5. Complementing
      6. Contradicting
      7. Deceiving - leakage
   E. Nonverbal Communication Is Ambiguous

IV. **TYPES OF NONVERBAL COMMUNICATION**
   A. Body Orientation
   B. Posture
      1. Forward/backward lean
      2. Tension/relaxation

   C. Gestures
      1. Illustrators
      2. Emblems
      3. Adaptors (manipulators)
   D. Face and Eyes
      1. Complexity
      2. Speed
      3. Microexpression
      4. Kinds of messages
         a. Involvement/avoidance
         b. Positive/negative attitude
         c. Dominance/submission
         d. Interest (pupil dilation)
   E. Voice (Paralanguage): Tone, Speed, Pitch, Volume, Number and Length of Pauses, Disfluencies
   F. Touch
      1. Increases liking
      2. Increases compliance
      3. Connected to health
   G. Physical Attractiveness
   H. Clothing
   I. Distance (proxemics)
      1. Intimate
      2. Personal
      3. Social
      4. Public
   J. Territoriality
   K. Physical Environment
   L. Time (Chronemics)

KEY TERMS

accenting
adaptors
body orientation
chronemics
complementing
contradicting
disfluencies
emblems
gestures
illustrators
intimate distance
kinesics
leakage

microexpression
mixed message
nonverbal communication
paralanguage
personal distance
posture
proxemics
public distance
regulating
repeating
social distance
substituting
territory

ACTIVITIES

6.1 DESCRIBING NONVERBAL STATES

❖ **Activity Type: Skill Builder**

Purpose

To describe the nonverbal behaviors that indicate various emotional and attitudinal states.

Instructions

NOTE: Group members (or individuals) may want to make videotaped examples of their own behavior reflecting each of the situations below or they may want to collect television or movie examples illustrating the emotions and attitudes described below.

1. For each of the statements below, record the nonverbal behaviors that reflect the attitude or emotions described.
2. Compare your responses with those of others in the class and note the similarities and differences in your responses.

Example 1

He says I'm too eager to please.

Take a little more time to respond after a request. Lean toward the person a little less. Smile, but don't keep the smile on your face continuously. Gesture, but don't gesture as quickly. Stand a little more erect and hold all the parts of your body more still.

Example 2

She listens well.

Turns body toward me, leans forward, smiles once or twice, nods, maintains eye contact about 80 percent of the time.

1. He's so mean.

_____

_____

_____

2. She says I don't talk nice to her.

_____

_____

_____

3. He's not into this.

_____

_____

_____

4. She can't stop flirting. (Use Table 6.2 from the text if you need help here.)

_____

_____

_____

5. They tell me I'm too tense.

_____

_____

_____

6. She acts like she's in charge.

_____

_____

_____

7. He makes a big deal of everything.

_____

_____

_____

8. You need to act more sure of yourself.

_____

_____

_____

9. He seems friendly.

_____

_____

_____

10. You're not exactly a ray of sunshine.

_____

_____

_____

11. They tell me I'm too aggressive.

_____

_____

_____

12. She's "hyper."

_____

_____

_____

List how at least two of the preceding statements could be taken in both positive and negative ways (*i.e., number 6 could be positive if you are grateful that she's organizing things, but negative if you're resentful of her influence*).

_____

_____

_____

_____

_____

List the nonverbal behaviors that are associated with the alternate interpretation (the one you didn't record initially) and your reaction. (*i.e., I can see the positive side of taking charge—assigning seating, standing erect, firm voice, keeping to a time schedule, nodding and making eye contact with those who should speak to you. There's often a small difference between the nonverbal behaviors I find positive and those I find annoying or bossy*).

_____

_____

_____

_____

_____

6.2 NONVERBAL HOW-TO'S

❖ Activity Type: Skill Builder

Purpose

To define what you and others in the class consider effective nonverbal behavior in some social situations.

Instructions

1. For each of the social situations below, list the nonverbal behaviors you believe will achieve the stated goal.
2. Compare your answers with those of others in your class.
3. Reflect on the behavior of yourself and others important to you. How might you change some of the nonverbal cues you display to communicate what you desire more effectively?

Example

Initiate conversation with a stranger at a party.
Make eye contact, offer hand in greeting, smile, come within four feet of other person, turn body toward other person, nod occasionally when other is talking.

1. Take control or exercise leadership in a class group.

   _____

   _____

2. Come across well in a job interview.

   _____

   _____

3. Tell an interesting joke or story.

   _____

   _____

4. Appear friendly and warm without "coming on too strong."

   _____

   _____

5. Signal your desire to leave a conversation when the other person keeps on talking.

   _____

   _____

6. Appear confident when asking boss for a raise.

_____

_____

7. Appear interested in class lecture.

_____

_____

8. Avoid talking with an undesirable person.

_____

_____

9. Show kindness toward an elderly relative.

_____

_____

10. Appear concerned about a friend's dilemma.

_____

_____

Describe someone's nonverbal behavior that you would like to change.

_____

_____

_____

_____

How would you tell them to change (if you thought they'd listen)?

_____

_____

_____

_____

_____

6.3 EVALUATING AMBIGUITY

◆ **Activity Type: Invitation to Insight**

Purpose

1. To analyze the verbal and nonverbal aspects of your communication behaviors.
2. To weigh the consequences of sending congruent versus ambiguous messages.

Instructions

1. In each of the following situations, describe verbal and nonverbal behaviors likely to occur. (nonverbal behaviors include: body orientation, posture, gesture, face and eyes, voice, touch, physical attractiveness, clothing, proxemics, territoriality, physical environment and time). Nonverbal behaviors seldom occur alone, so describe clusters of at least 3 nonverbal behaviors for each situation. Note whether the verbal and nonverbal behaviors are ambiguous or congruent (congruent means they send the same, consistent message). Finally, evaluate the possible consequences of the ambiguity or congruency.
2. Next describe situations from your own life and how you would send verbal and nonverbal messages. Include the possible consequences of your congruent or ambiguous behaviors.
3. After you've completed the examples, answer the questions about congruency/ambiguity.

SITUATION	YOUR VERBAL BEHAVIOR	YOUR NONVERBAL BEHAVIOR (USE A **CLUSTER** OF BEHAVIORS HERE)	ARE THE BEHAVIORS AMBIGUOUS?	POSSIBLE CONSEQUENCES
Example *Person I like a lot takes me out to dinner and I have a good time and enjoy the food.*	*"I'm really enjoying this; the food is terrific and so is the company."*	*I look at my partner when I talk, smiling and tilting my head, and leaning slightly forward. I touch my partner light on the arm and hand.*	*My verbal and nonverbal behaviors are congruent, not ambiguous.*	*I hope my partner will understand how much I care and enjoy our time together. I run the risk of being hurt if my partner's feelings don't match mine, but I'm willing to take that risk.*
1. My boss asks me to work late when I've made other plans.				
2. My roommate asks, while I'm doing homework, if I can make dinner.				

SITUATION	YOUR VERBAL BEHAVIOR	YOUR NONVERBAL BEHAVIOR (USE A CLUSTER OF BEHAVIORS HERE)	ARE THE BEHAVIORS AMBIGUOUS?	POSSIBLE CONSEQUENCES
3. My relative drops in to visit me when other people are over for the evening.				
4. My romantic partner says I act like I'm indifferent when we discuss our future.				
5. Our waiter grabs my plate and asks if I'm finished while food is still on my plate.				
6. (your example)				
7. (your example)				
8. (your example)				

Class _____   Name _____

Consider situations in addition to the examples in this exercise when answering the following questions.

In what situations should you express yourself ambiguously? Explain how sending one message verbally and another one nonverbally could be beneficial.

_____

_____

_____

_____

Describe situations in which ambiguity is not desirable. Describe how you could best match your verbal and nonverbal behaviors in these situations.

_____

_____

_____

_____

_____

_____

Chapter Six

6.4 MEDIATED MESSAGES – NONVERBAL

◆❖ Activity Type: Group Discussion

Purpose

To analyze nonverbal communication in mediated contexts.

Instructions

Discuss each of the questions below in your group. Prepare written answers for your instructor, or be prepared to contribute to a large group discussion, comparing your experiences with those of others in your class.

1. Mediated contexts often deprive us of important nonverbal communication cues. Discuss what nonverbal cues are present and absent in the mediated contexts (e.g., telephone, email, handwritten messages) used by members of your group.

   _____

   _____

2. List substitutions that people make for missing nonverbal cues (i.e., facial expressions, tone of voice, touch, spacing) in mediated contexts. How effective are these substitutions?

   _____

   _____

3. Your textbook discusses nonverbal signals of deception, or leakage. Describe why you think it is easier or more difficult to detect deception in mediated contexts.

   _____

   _____

4. Discuss the messages conveyed by the use of time in mediated contexts (for example, the length of time taken to return a phone call or an email). Include both intentional and unintentional messages.

   _____

   _____

5. On *InfoTrac*, read *Mind your e-mail manners*, from the Journal of Accountancy. List the two most useful pieces of advice here. Explain why you find them useful.

   _____

   _____

6.5 YOUR CALL – NONVERBAL

◆❖ Activity Type: Group Discussion

Purpose

To analyze the possible interpretations of nonverbal behavior and how to respond to them.

Instructions

Use the case below and the discussion questions that follow to discuss the variety of communication issues involved in effective communication. Make notes on this page, add other pages on your own, or prepare a group report/analysis based on your discussion. Add your own experiences to individualize the analysis to make it **Your Call**.

Case

Malena and Dolly are coworkers in different departments in a large company. Over coffee one day Malena tells Dolly that she's been feeling very uneasy lately about her boss's behavior. "I'm not exactly sure how to describe it," Malena says, "but I think he's 'coming on' to me, and I don't know what to do."

1. If Malena decides to report this behavior, she needs to be able to describe it. Imagine a situation like this and describe the probable behavior of Malena's boss.

     _____

     _____

2. Explain how Malena might be misinterpreting her boss's behavior.

     _____

     _____

3. Describe nonverbal behaviors on Malena's part that might contribute to the problem.

     _____

     _____

4. If you were Dolly, what would you tell Malena to do verbally and nonverbally to handle this issue?

     _____

     _____

5. On InfoTrac, read *"SEXUAL HARASSMENT: HANDLING THE COMPLAINT" AND "SEXUAL HARASSMENT: UNDERSTANDING THE LAW"*. How would you change your answers above after reading this article?

     _____

     _____

Chapter Six

6.6 DEAR PROFESSOR – RELATIONAL RESPONSES

◆❖ Activity Type: Invitation to Insight/Group Discussion

Purposes

1. To examine communication challenges addressed by this chapter.
2. To demonstrate your ability to analyze communication challenges using the concepts in this chapter.

Instructions

1. Read the Dear Professor letter and response below.
2. Discuss ProfMary's response. Would you add anything or give a different response?
3. Read the second letter. Construct an answer to it, <u>using terms and concepts from this chapter.</u> <u>Underline or boldface the terms and concepts you apply here.</u>
4. If class structure permits, share your letters and answers with other members of the class.

Part A - The letter

Dear Professor,

My roommate keeps borrowing my clothes without asking, and I want her to stop. I've confronted her a few times, but she still goes into my room and my closet and takes them. Then I have to go look for them when I want to wear them. She's insensitive to my needs. What should I do? **Erline**

The response

Dear Erline,

*You and your roommate need to get a mutual understanding of your **territory**. It sounds as if you do not want her to even go in your room, let alone your closet, but she doesn't understand that (or perhaps doesn't want to). **Clothing** is a personal ownership thing for you, and you resent your roommate invading your **space** and taking your personal items.*

*Provided you don't invade your roommate's **space** in some way (so that your roommate feels justified in taking your things), it's time to describe what you consider your space and your things, what you consider her space and her things, and what you share as roommates. You need to have this talk in a calm **tone of voice**, not accusing your roommate of atrocities, but simply describing the boundaries, as you see them. **Smile** at your roommate and invite feedback by **nodding** or **gesturing**.*

Compile a list of things you could do so that each of you respects the other's space and things. On that list could be locking your door or closet (with the hope that you won't have to go that far). Don't make threats. Explain how important your clothes are to you and how you don't want this borrowing thing to come between you as roommates since everything else about your living together is so good. If you get her to buy into the problem-solving, she'll be more likely to comply with your desires about your clothes.

In hopes for your relational satisfaction,   *ProfMary*

Part B - The letter

Dear Professor,
My father always answers my questions with only "yes" or "no" — "Sorry, I don't have time." It is as if he doesn't want to address my concerns. But then he'll come to me at the worst time (like when I'm in the middle of studying for an exam) and say things like, "So, how's it going?" So, basically, we never talk. Is there anything I can do to make him see how he's cutting me off from him? ***Kevin***

Your response

Dear Kevin,

_____

_____

_____

_____

_____

_____

_____

_____

_____

_____

_____

_____

Study Guide

CHECK YOUR UNDERSTANDING

Crossword Puzzle

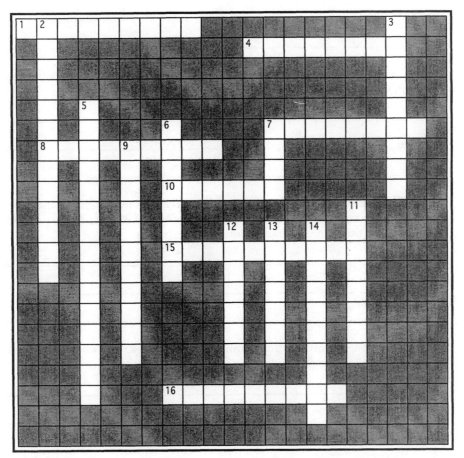

ACROSS

1. a nonverbal function that emphasizes part of a verbal message
4. Hall's spatial zone from skin contact to 18 inches
7. a nonverbal function that manages whose turn it is to talk
8. nonverbal behavior cues that signal the untruthfulness of a verbal message
10. a deliberate nonverbal behavior with precise meaning known to virtually all members of a cultural group
15. the study of how humans use and structure time
16. the study of how people and animals use space

DOWN

2. nonverbal behavior that is inconsistent with a verbal message
3. a geographical area to which we assume some kind of "rights"
5. brief facial expressions
6. the study of body position and motion
7. an example of a personal territory within a house
9. nonverbal behavior that accompanies and supports verbal messages
11. movements of the hands and arms
12. the way in which individuals carry themselves: erect, slumping, etc.
13. nonverbal behaviors that reveal information a communicator does not disclose verbally
14. a nonlinguistic verbalization like um, er, ah

True/False

Mark the statements below as true or false. Correct statements that are false on the lines below to create a true statement.

_____ 1. Nonverbal behaviors are, by their nature, intentional.

_____

_____

_____

_____ 2. Certain nonverbal behaviors like smiling are universal, and thus they are used and interpreted similarly around the world.

_____

_____

_____

_____ 3. The concept of nonverbal convergence illustrates that skilled communicators can adapt their behavior when interacting with members of other cultures or subcultures in order to make the exchange more smooth and effective.

_____

_____

_____

_____ 4. Nonverbal communication is much better suited to expressing attitudes and feelings than it is to expressing ideas.

_____

_____

_____

_____ 5. Research on nonverbal communication and lying shows that individuals who are trying to deceive others are less likely to show nonverbal evidence of lying if they haven't had a chance to rehearse their lying and when they feel strongly about the information being hidden.

_____

_____

_____

_____ 6. In studies of detecting lying, men are consistently more accurate than women at detecting the lies and discovering the underlying truth.

_____

_____

_____

_____ 7. Both verbal and nonverbal messages are communicated one at a time, rather like pearls on a string.

_____

_____

_____

_____ 8. Unlike verbal communication that is intermittent (starts and stops), nonverbal communication is continuous and never ending.

_____

_____

_____

_____ 9. The nonverbal impact of messages is more powerful than the verbal impact.

_____

_____

_____

_____ 10. Nonverbal communication is clearer than verbal communication.

_____

_____ 11. Females are more nonverbally expressive than males, and they are better at recognizing others' nonverbal behavior.

_____

_____

_____

_____ 12. The main reason we miss most posture messages is that they are so obvious.

_____

_____

_____

_____ 13. Behaviors that have one meaning for members of the same culture or co-culture can be interpreted differently by members of another group.

_____ 14. Women are more likely to fall for the deception of an intimate partner than are men.

_____ 15. Nonverbal messages are clearer than verbal messages in matters of sexual consent.

Completion

Fill in the blanks below with the correct terms chosen from the list below.

illustrator	intimate	personal	social	public	relaxation
	paralanguage	emblem	adaptor	touch	body
orientation	nonverbal learning disorder				

1. _____ is the distance zone identified by Hall that ranges from four to about twelve feet; within it are the kinds of communication that usually occur in business.

2. _____ is a postural cue such as leaning back or lowering shoulders that a higher status person usually exhibits when not feeling threatened.

3. _____ is a deliberate, nonverbal behavior that has a very precise meaning known to virtually everyone within a cultural group.

4. _____ is the distance zone identified by Hall that ranges from eighteen inches to four feet and includes behavior found in most social conversations.

5. _____ is a gesture that accompanies speech but doesn't stand on its own.

6. _____ is the degree to which we face toward or away from someone with our body, feet, and head.

7. _____ is the distance zone identified by Hall that ranges from skin contact to about eighteen inches; we usually use this distance with people in private who are emotionally very close to us.

8. _____ is the distance zone identified by Hall that ranges from twelve feet outward and includes communication such as that found in a typical classroom.

9. _____ is nonverbal behavior that includes having a foreign accent.

10. _____ is nonverbal behavior that includes brushing up against someone.

11. _____ is an unconscious body movement that helps us adjust to the environment.

12. _____ is a syndrome that makes reading nonverbal cues more difficult.

Multiple Choice

Choose the letter of the type of nonverbal communication that is illustrated below.

a. environment   b. paralinguistics   c. proxemics   d. territoriality

_____   1. No one dared to sit in Ralph's chair.

_____   2. Jeremy put a "NO ENTRANCE" sign on his door.

_____   3. The students rearranged the chairs in the classroom.

_____   4. Manuela stepped back three feet from her friend.

_____   5. The lovers were sitting only inches apart.

_____   6. Rob's voice softened when he spoke to her.

_____   7. There was a long pause after the decision was made.

_____   8. Mitchell sighed audibly.

_____   9. Gretchen took the third seat down from Yayoi.

_____ 10. Kevin was annoyed that someone was leaning on his car.

a. body orientation   b. gesture   c. touch   d. face and eyes

_____ 11. The children playfully kicked one another.

_____ 12. Professor Jimenez illustrated her lecture with many arm movements.

_____ 13. Leland shifted his shoulders toward the speaker.

_____ 14. Ernie avoided looking at her.

_____ 15. The executive stared at her employee.

_____ 16. Martin turned his body away from his brother.

_____ 17. The officer pointed in the correct direction.

_____ 18. Letoya didn't appreciate the slap on the back.

_____ 19. Blake set his jaw in disgust.

_____ 20. Francesca signaled "OK" across the room.

Chapter Six

CHAPTER 6 STUDY GUIDE ANSWERS

Crossword Puzzle

```
 1a c c e n t i n g                              3t
    o                        4i n t i m a t e     e
    n                                             r
    t                                             r
    r      5m              6k        7r e g u l a t e
    a       i               k        o            o
   8d e c e i v i n g        r        o            r
    i      r    9l           n       o            y
    c      o    l          10e m b l e m
    t      e    u           s              11g
    i      x    s           i      12p 13l 14d e
    n      p    t          15c h r o n e m i c s
    g      r    r           s      s   a   s   u
           e    a               t   k   f   r
           s    t               u   a   l   e
           s    o               r   g   u   s
           i    r               e   e   e
           o                            n
          16n              p r o x e m i c s
                                        y
```

True/False

1. F	4. T	7. F	10. F	13. T
2. T	5. F	8. T	11. T	14. T
3. T	6. F	9. T	12. F	15. F

Completion

1. social
2. relaxation
3. emblem
4. personal
5. illustrator
6. body orientation
7. intimate
8. public
9. paralanguage
10. touch
11. adaptor
12. nonverbal learning disorder

Multiple choice

1. d	5. c	9. c	13. a	17. b
2. d	6. b	10. d	14. d	18. c
3. a	7. b	11. c	15. d	19. d
4. c	8. b	12. b	16. a	20. b

Nonverbal Communication

Chapter Six

CHAPTER SEVEN

LISTENING: MORE THAN MEETS THE EAR

OUTLINE

Use this outline to take notes as you read the chapter in the text or as your instructor lectures in class.

I. **LISTENING IS IMPORTANT**
  A. **Most Frequent Communication Activity**
  B. **Valued Relational Skill**
  C. **Important to Career Success**

II. **ELEMENTS IN THE LISTENING PROCESS**
  A. **Hearing - Physiological**
  B. **Attending - Psychological**
  C. **Understanding – Making Sense**
  D. **Responding – Observable Feedback**
  E. **Remembering - Recalling**

III. **THE CHALLENGE OF LISTENING**
  A. **Types of ineffective listening**
    1. Pseudolistening
    2. Stage Hogging
    3. Selective Listening
    4. Insulated Listening
    5. Defensive Listening
    6. Ambushing
    7. Insensitive Listening
  B. **Why we don't listen better**
    1. Message Overload
    2. Preoccupation
    3. Rapid Thought
    4. Effort
    5. External Noise
    6. Hearing Problems
    7. Faulty Assumptions
    8. Lack of Apparent Advantages
    9. Lack of Training
    10. Media Influences
  C. **Meeting the challenge of listening better**
    1. Talk Less
    2. Get Rid of Distractions
    3. Don't Judge Prematurely
    4. Look for Key Ideas

IV. **TYPES OF LISTENING RESPONSES**
  A. **Prompting: encouraging**
  B. **Questioning: clarifying**
    1. Avoid counterfeit questions that
      a. trap the speaker
      b. make statements
      c. carry hidden agendas
      d. seek "correct" answers
      e. are based on unchecked assumptions
    2. Ask sincere questions
  C. **Paraphrasing: reflecting understanding**
    1. Factual information
    2. Personal information
      a.. Change the speaker's wording
      b. Offer an example of what you think the speaker is talking about
      c. Reflect the underlying theme of the speaker's remarks
    3. Remain tentative
    4. Use sparingly
      a. If the problem is complex enough
      b. If you have necessary time and concern
      c. If you are genuinely interested in helping
      d. If you can withhold judgment
      e. Make paraphrasing proportional to other types
  D. **Supporting: expressing solidarity**
    1. Types
      a. Agreement
      b. Offers to help
      c. Praise
      d. Reassurance
      e. Diversion

2. Potential problems
   a. Deny others the right to their feelings
   b. minimize the significance of the situation
   c. focus on "then and there" rather than "here and now"
   d. cast judgment
   e. defend yourself
3. Guidelines
   a. Approval not necessary
   b. Monitor reaction
   c. Support not always welcome

E. **Analyzing: interpreting**
   1. Be tentative
   2. Have chance of being correct
   3. Receptive other
   4. Motivated to be helpful

F. **Advising: offering a solution**
   1. Be accurate
   2. Be sure other is ready to accept
   3. Best if blame is not likely
   4. Deliver supportively, in a face-saving manner

G. **Judging: evaluating**
   1. Be sure judgment is asked for
   2. Be genuinely constructive

H. **Choosing the best listening response**
   1. Gender
   2. The situation
   3. The other person
   4. Your personal style

KEY TERMS

advising response
ambushing
analyzing response
attending
counterfeit questions
defensive listening
hearing
insensitive listening
insulated listening
judging response
listening
paraphrasing

prompting
pseudolistening
questioning response
remembering
responding
selective listening
sincere questions
stage-hogging
supportive response
understanding

ACTIVITIES

7.1 LISTENING DIARY

◆ Activity Type: Invitation to Insight

Purposes

1. To identify the styles of listening you use in your interpersonal relationships.
2. To discover the consequences of the listening styles you use.

Background

Looking Out/Looking In identifies several styles of effective and ineffective listening that you can use when seeking information from another:

pseudolistening	insensitive listening
stage hogging	ambushing
selective listening	prompting
insulated listening	questioning
defensive listening	paraphrasing

Instructions

1. Use the following form to record the listening styles you use in various situations.
2. After completing your diary, record your conclusions.

TIME AND PLACE	PEOPLE	SUBJECT	LISTENING STYLE(S)	CONSEQUENCES
Example *Saturday night party*	*My date and several new acquaintances*	*Good backpacking trips*	*Stage-hogging: I steered everybody's remarks around to my own experiences*	*I guess I was trying to get everyone to like me, but my egotistical attitude probably accomplished the opposite.*
1.				
2.				

TIME AND PLACE	PEOPLE	SUBJECT	LISTENING STYLE(S)	CONSEQUENCES
3.				
4.				

Based on your observations, what styles of effective and ineffective listening do you use most often? In what situations do you use each of these styles? (Consider the people involved, the time, subject, and your personal mood when determining situational variables.)

_____

_____

_____

_____

What are the consequences of using the listening styles you have just described?

_____

_____

_____

_____

7.2 EFFECTIVE QUESTIONING

❖ **Activity Type: Skill Builder**

Purpose

To develop your ability to question effectively in order to gain information about another person's thoughts.

Instructions

1. For each of the following statements, write two questions to get more information. Avoid counterfeit questions that trap the speaker, carry hidden agendas, seek "correct" answers, or are based on unchecked assumptions.
2. Enter statement examples of your own and two questions each to solicit information.

Example

"It's not fair that I have to work so much. Other students can get better grades because they have the time to study."
How do you feel when others score higher than you?
How many hours a week do you work?

1. "I guess it's OK for you to use my computer, but you have to understand that I've put a lot of time and money into it."

   _____

   _____

2. "You'll have the best chance at getting a loan for the new car you want if you give us a complete financial statement and credit history."

   _____

   _____

3. (Instructor to student) "This paper shows a lot of promise. It could probably earn you an A grade if you just develop the idea about the problems that arise from poor listening a bit more."

   _____

   _____

4. "I do like the communication course, but it's not at all what I expected. It's much more *personal*, if you know what I mean."

   _____

   _____

5. "We just got started on your car's transmission. I'm pretty sure we can have it ready tonight."

_____

_____

6. "I do think it's wrong to take any lives, but sometimes I think certain criminals deserve capital punishment."

_____

_____

7. "My son never tells me what's going on in his life. And now he's moving away."

_____

_____

8. "My family is so controlling. They make it impossible for me to escape."

_____

_____

9. "It was a great game, I guess.   I played a lot, but only scored once. The coach put Ryan in ahead of me."

_____

_____

10. "We had a great evening last night. The dinner was fantastic; so was the party. We saw lots of people. Erin loves that sort of thing."

_____

_____

11. (Your example)_____

_____

_____

12. (Your example)_____

_____

_____

7.3 PARAPHRASING

◆❖ **Activity Type: Skill Builder**

Purpose

To create paraphrasing responses to others' problems.

Background

The most helpful paraphrasing responses reflect both the speaker's thoughts and feelings. In order for this style of helping to be effective, you also have to sound like yourself, and not another person or a robot. There are many ways to reflect another's thoughts and feelings:

"It sounds like you're . . ."   "And so . . . "
"I hear you saying . . ."   "Is it that . . . "
"Let me see if I've got it. You're saying . . ."   "Are you . . ."
"So you're telling me . . ."   "Could you mean . . . "

Leave your paraphrase open (tentative) by using words that invite the speaker to clarify or correct your paraphrase (ex: "Is that right?")

Instructions

Write a paraphrasing response for each of the statements that follow. Be sure that the response fits your style of speaking, while at the same time it reflects the speaker's *thoughts* and *feelings*.

Example

"Stan always wants to tell me about the women he's going out with; he gives me `blow-by-blow' descriptions of their dates that take hours, and he never seems to ask about who I'm going out with or what I'm interested in."

"It seems like you might be tired (feeling) of hearing about Stan's love life (thoughts) and maybe a little put-out (feeling) that he doesn't solicit information from you about whom you're dating (thoughts)— is that it?"

1. "I hate this instructor. First she told me my paper was too short, so I gave her more information. Now she tells me it's too wordy."

    _____

    _____

    _____

2. "I worked up that whole study—did all the surveying, the compiling, the writing. It was my idea in the first place. But he turned it in to the head office with his name on it, and he got the credit."

    _____

    _____

    _____

3. "We can't decide whether to put Grandmother in a nursing home. She hates the idea, but she can't take care of herself anymore, and it's just too much for us."

_____

_____

_____

4. "She believed everything he said about me. She wouldn't even listen to my side—just started yelling at me. I thought we were better friends than that."

_____

_____

_____

5. "I'm really starting to hate my job. Every day I do the same boring, mindless work. But if I quit, I might not find any better work."

_____

_____

_____

6. "My girlfriend hasn't called me in forever. I think she must be mad at me."

_____

_____

_____

7. "How can I tell him how I really feel? He might get mad, and then we'd start arguing. He'll think I don't love him if I tell him my real feelings. I'm at a loss."

_____

_____

_____

8. "Why don't you try to be a little less messy around here? This place looks like a dump to all our friends."

_____

_____

_____

9. "There's no reasoning with him. All he cares about is his image—not all the work I have to do to cover for him."

_____

_____

_____

10. "You'd think someone who loves you would take off to be with you now and then, wouldn't you?"

_____

_____

_____

11. "Computers are supposed to save time? That's a joke."

_____

_____

_____

12. "He acts as if staying home with two children all day is easy. I'm more tired now than when I worked full-time – and I got paid then!"

_____

_____

_____

13. "My father is so needy since my mother died. I have no life of my own any more."

_____

_____

_____

14. "Group projects are a nightmare. There should be a waning sign for classes that require them."

_____

_____

_____

7.4 LISTENING CHOICES

❖ **Activity Type: Skill Builder**

Purpose

To practice different listening styles in responding to others.

Instructions

For each of the problem statements below, write a response in each style of helping discussed in *Looking Out/Looking In*. Make your response as realistic as possible. Then record a situation of your own and write listening responses for it.

Example

"I don't know what to do. I tried to explain to my professor why the assignment was late, but he wouldn't even listen to me."
Prompting (*Short silence*) *And so . . . ? (Look expectantly at partner).*
Questioning *What did he say? Can you make up the assignment? How do you feel about this?*
Paraphrasing *You sound really discouraged, since he didn't even seem to care about your reasons—is that it?*
Supporting *All of your work has been so good that I'm sure this one assignment won't matter. Don't worry!*
Analyzing *I think the reason he wasn't sympathetic is because he hears lots of excuses this time of year.*
Advising *You ought to write him a note. He might be more open if he has time to read it and think about it.*
Judging *You have to accept these things. Moping won't do any good, so quit feeling sorry for yourself.*

1. My girlfriend says she wants to date other guys this summer while I'm away, working construction. She claims it's just to keep busy and that it won't make any difference with us, but I think she wants to break off permanently, and she's trying to do it gently.

    Prompting _____

    Questioning _____

    _____

    Paraphrasing _____

    _____

    Supporting _____

    _____

    Analyzing _____

    _____

    Advising _____

    _____

Judging _____

_____

2. My roommate and I can't seem to get along. She's always having her boyfriend over, and he doesn't know when to go home. I don't want to move out, but I can't put up with this much longer. If I bring it up I know my roommate will get defensive, though.

Prompting _____

Questioning _____

_____

Paraphrasing _____

_____

Supporting _____

_____

Analyzing _____

_____

Advising _____

_____

Judging _____

_____

3. What do you do about a friend who borrows things and doesn't return them?

Prompting _____

Questioning _____

_____

Paraphrasing _____

_____

Supporting _____

_____

Analyzing _____

_____

Advising _____

_____

Judging _____

_____

4. The pressure of going to school and doing all the other things in my life is really getting to me. I can't go on like this, but I don't know where I can cut back.

Prompting _____

Questioning _____

_____

Paraphrasing _____

_____

Supporting _____

_____

Analyzing _____

_____

Advising _____

_____

Judging _____

_____

5. You think that by the time you become an adult your parents would stop treating you like a child, but not mine! If I wanted their advice about how to live my life, I'd ask.

Prompting _____

Questioning _____

_____

Paraphrasing _____

_____

Supporting _____

_____

Analyzing _____

_____

Advising _____

_____

Judging _____

_____

6. (record a situation of your own here) _____

_____

Prompting _____

Questioning _____

_____

Paraphrasing _____

_____

Supporting _____

_____

Analyzing _____

_____

Advising _____

_____

Judging _____

_____

7.5 INFORMATIONAL LISTENING

❖ Activity Type: Skill Builder

Instructions

1. Join with three partners to create a foursome. Label the members A, B, C, and D.
2. A and B review the list below, choosing the topic upon which they disagree most widely.
3. A and B conduct a five-minute conversation on the topic they have chosen. During this period, the speakers may not express their own ideas until they have effectively questioned and then paraphrased the other person's position to his or her satisfaction. (If A and B finish discussing one item, they should move on to a second one from the list below.)
   C observes A   D observes B
4. At the end of the conversation, the observers should review the listening with the persons they observed.
5. Repeat steps 1–5 with the roles of conversationalists and observers reversed.

Topics

Indicate your position on each statement below by circling one of the following labels:

TA = totally agree   A = agree   D = disagree   TD = totally disagree

1. Despite the value of classes like this one, in the
   last analysis, good communicators are born, not made.   **TA   A   D   TD**

2. One measure of a person's effectiveness as a communicator
   is how well he or she is liked by others.   **TA   A   D   TD**

3. No matter how unreasonable or rude they are, people
   deserve to be treated with respect.   **TA   A   D   TD**

4. An effective communicator should be able to handle any
   any situation in a way that leaves the other person feeling
   positive about the interaction.   **TA   A   D   TD**

5. Interpersonal communication classes should be a
   required part of everyone's college education.   **TA   A   D   TD**

6. Most of what is taught in interpersonal communication
   classes is really just common sense.   **TA   A   D   TD**

OR as an alternative

1. Choose a topic of interest to you and a partner (music, politics, religion, men, women, morals, etc.). It is best if you anticipate some difference of opinion on the topic.

2. Take turns stating your opinion. The only rule is that before you can take your turn stating your opinion, you must effectively question and paraphrase the content of your partner's opinion to his or her satisfaction.

Chapter Seven

7.6 LISTENING AND RESPONDING STYLES

❖ Activity Type: Oral Skill

Purpose

To give you practice in using different listening styles to enhance listening effectiveness.

Instructions

1. With a partner, decide on communication situations that require effective listening. The situations should be real for the person describing them and might involve a problem, a decision that needs to be made, an issue of importance, or a change in a relationship.
2. Have your partner tell you the problem/issue/decision/relationship while you listen effectively.
3. You then tell your partner of your problem/issue/decision/relationship while your partner listens effectively.
4. Analyze the listening styles you used. Which were most/least effective in this situation? Which styles do you need to work on?
5. Use the checklist below to evaluate listening effectiveness.

Checklist

Uses appropriate language and nonverbal behaviors that   _____
   -demonstrate genuine interest
   -seem compatible with your personal communication style

Uses a balance of the following types of helping responses, as appropriate   _____

   <u>For both understanding and supporting</u>
   Prompting   _____
   genuine questions   _____
   paraphrasing   _____
      concisely and clearly reflects speaker's *thoughts*   _____
      concisely and clearly reflects speaker's *feelings*   _____
      requests confirmation of paraphrase accuracy   _____

<u>For supporting only (as appropriate)</u>
   Analyzing   _____
   Advising   _____
   supporting (comforting, praising, agreeing, humor)   _____

Based on self-observation (class feedback, videotape, etc.) and personal reflection analyzes _____

_____

_____

   Which listening styles did you rely on most in this situation?   _____
   Which listening styles were most/least effective in this situation?   _____
   Which combination of responses could you have used in this situation, and which could you use in the future to be most effective?   _____

                                                Total   _____

7.7 MEDIATED MESSAGES – LISTENING

❖ Activity Type: Group Discussion

Purpose

To analyze listening behaviors in mediated contexts.

Instructions

Discuss each of the questions below in your group. Prepare written answers for your instructor, or be prepared to contribute to a large group discussion, comparing your experiences with those of others in your class.

1. Media influences our listening or nonlistening (e.g. the brief segments we have become accustomed to on radio and television discourage focused listening). Record difficulties (focusing, attention span) that your group members have experienced with media in the listening process.

_____

_____

_____

2. Describe ineffective listening styles (pseudolistening, selective, defensive, etc.) that your group thinks are more predominant in mediated contexts.

_____

_____

_____

3. Describe how some listening may be done more effectively through mediated channels.

_____

_____

_____

4. Through your InfoTrac connection, read about the listening skills of managers in: *Is anybody listening* by Alexander Hiam (*Training*, August 1997). Record your reactions here:

_____

_____

_____

Chapter Seven

7.8 YOUR CALL – LISTENING

❖ **Activity Type: Group Discussion**

Purpose

To evaluate the appropriateness of different listening styles in a relationship.

Instructions

Use the case below and the discussion questions that follow to discuss the variety of communication issues involved in effective communication. Make notes on this page, add other pages on your own, or prepare a group report/analysis based on your discussion. Add your own experiences to individualize the analysis to make it **Your Call.**

Case

Arleen and Valerie have been friends since elementary school and are now in their thirties. Valerie has been happily married for ten years. Arleen has been engaged four times, and each time has broken it off as the marriage date approaches. Valerie has listened, mainly questioning, supporting, and paraphrasing. Arleen has just announced another engagement.

1. Valerie wants to give Arleen advice this time. What should she say?

   _____

   _____

2. Since Valerie has known Arleen for so long, she's considering an analyzing style. What would she say? What would be the effect of analyzing versus advising on the relationship?

   _____

   _____

   _____

3. What listening style(s) do you think would be most helpful to Arleen? Construct a response for Valerie using that style.

   _____

   _____

   _____

4. Suppose that the two friends described here are both men. How would your responses to the preceding questions change?

   _____

   _____

   _____

7.9 DEAR PROFESSOR – RELATIONAL RESPONSES

◆◆ Activity Type: Invitation to Insight/Group Discussion

Purposes

1. To examine communication challenges addressed by this chapter.
2. To demonstrate your ability to analyze communication challenges using the concepts in this chapter.

Instructions

1. Read the Dear Professor letter and response below.
2. Discuss ProfMary's response. Would you add anything or give a different response?
3. Read the second letter. Construct an answer to it, <u>using terms and concepts from this chapter.</u> <u>Underline or boldface the terms and concepts you apply here.</u>
4. Before you construct your response to the second letter, use your InfoTrac connection to read *Love lessons: 6 new moves to improve your relationship* by Hara Estroff Marano in *Psychology Today* (March-April 1997, Vol. 30, #2, p. 40). It includes advice on listening.
5. If class structure permits, share your letters and answers with other members of the class.

Part A - The letter

Dear Professor,

My mother wants and expects all of her adult children (there are five of us) to call her all the time, and she gets upset if we don't. She won't call us, but when we call, she wants us to tell her all that we're doing in minute detail. She gets hurt and pouty if we don't share our lives with her, but when we start to tell her things, she doesn't really listen—as if she doesn't really want to hear from us after all.

*If I ask my mother about one of my siblings, she'll say, "I don't know; it's none of my business; I'm only the mother; it's up to them to let me know" as if I'm invading their privacy. But if I don't ask about them, she accuses me of not caring about my brothers and sisters. I'm getting so many mixed signals that I'm about ready to give up calling altogether. **Naomi***

The response

Dear Naomi,

Choosing the best listening responses in this situation will require a lot of reflection on your part. ***Consider the situation, your mother and your own comfort with different listening styles*** *to determine what to do. It is probable that you will not change your mother's communication behavior dramatically at this point, so you need to decide if you have enough patience and love to deal with her the way she is.*

*It is likely that **prompting, sincere questioning, and paraphrasing** are your best options. Your mother's insistence that you call her is probably to relieve her loneliness, so she wants to keep you on the phone to tell you about what is going on with her. You could ask **questions** like, "What did you do this morning?" or "How are you feeling today?" Whatever she says, you can **prompt** for more ("Oh, that's good/too bad/interesting – tell me more").   In addition, try to **paraphase her thoughts and feelings**. Don't **judge** her or your siblings. If she asks a question and doesn't listen to your response, you might listen to her first and then say, "You asked me about how my work was going, but I didn't get a chance to finish telling you about it. Do you have time now or would you like me to tell you another day when we have more time?" She might realize that she's cut you off and be more ready to listen. She may not.*

Given your relationship with your mother, you may have to be the more giving listener. If you are willing, you might feel good yourself for providing a good ear for your mother.

*In hopes for your relational satisfaction,   **ProfMary***

Part B - The letter

Dear Professor,
      Whenever I tell my friend a problem, she immediately says, "Well, when I was in that situation, I did this or that or . . . ." –completely ignoring my own problem and making it her issue. I care about this friend, but I want her to listen to ME. How can I explain this nicely?   ***Shane***

Your response

Dear Shane,

_____

_____

_____

_____

_____

_____

_____

_____

_____

_____

_____

_____

Study Guide

CHECK YOUR UNDERSTANDING

Crossword Puzzle

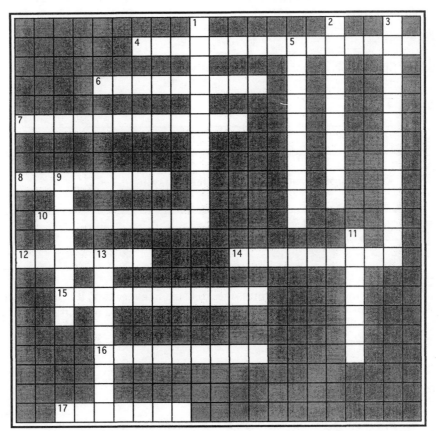

ACROSS

4. an imitation of true listening in which the receiver's mind is elsewhere
6. a response style in which the receiver perceives a speaker's comments as an attack
7. restating a speaker's thoughts and feelings in the listener's own words
8. a helping response in which the receiver offers suggestions about how the speaker should deal with a problem
10. using silences and brief statements of encouragement to draw out a speaker
12. the physiological dimension of listening
14. a response style in which the receiver responds only to messages that interest him or her
15. an ineffective listening style in which the listener accepts the speaker's words at face value, resulting in failure to recognize the thoughts or feelings that are not directly expressed by the speaker

16. a listening response that offers an interpretation of a speaker's message
17. a reaction in which the receiver evaluates the sender's message either favorably or unfavorably

DOWN

1. a style of listening in which the receiver seeks additional information from the sender
2. giving observable feedback to the speaker
3. occurs when sense is made of a message
5. a response style in which the receiver reassures, comforts, or distracts the person seeking help
9. a response in which the words of the speaker are repeated
11. a type of question that honestly seeks information without leading the speaker
13. an ineffective listening style in which the receiver ignores undesirable information

True/False

Mark the statements below as true or false. On the lines below each statement, correct the false statements by making a true statement.

_____ 1. We spend more time listening to others than in any other type of communication.

_____

_____

_____

_____ 2. Speaking is active; listening is passive.

_____

_____

_____

_____ 3. All interruptions are attempts at stage-hogging.

_____

_____

_____

_____ 4. Given the onslaught of messages to listen to every day, it is understandable (and perhaps even justifiable) to use pseudolistening and other nonlistening responses.

_____

_____

_____

_____ 5. In careful listening, the heart rate quickens and respiration increases.

_____

_____

_____

_____ 6. People speak at about the same rate as others are capable of understanding their speech.

_____

_____

_____

_____ 7. The advantages of listening are more obvious to people than the advantages of speaking.

_____

_____

_____

_____   8.   Paraphrasing is the most accurate listening response you can make.

_____

_____

_____

_____   9.   Judging as a listening response may be favorable or negative.

_____

_____

_____

_____   10.   Even an accurate form of analytic listening can create defensiveness since it may imply
superiority and evaluativeness.

_____

_____

_____

Completion

Fill in the blanks below with the correct terms chosen from the list below.

residual message	attending	conversational narcissist
sincere question	counterfeit question	constructive criticism
agreement	understanding	remembering
hearing	selective	insulated

1.   _____ is a name given to a nonlistening stage-hog.

2.   _____ is a genuine request for new information aimed at understanding
others.

3.   _____ is the information we store (remember) after processing information
from teachers, friends, radio, TV, and other sources.

4.   _____ is the psychological process of listening.

5.   _____ is a query that is a disguised attempt to send a message, not receive
one.

6.   _____ is a lesser form of negative judgment which is intended to help the
problem-holder improve in the future.

7. _____ is the physiological process of listening.

8. _____ is the process of making sense of a message.

9. _____ is the ability to recall information.

10. _____ is a listening response designed to show solidarity with speakers by telling them how right they are.

11. _____ is a nonlistening style that responds only to what the listener cares about.

12. _____ is a nonlistening style that ignores information the listener doesn't to deal with.

Multiple Choice

Match the letter of the listening type with its example found below.

a. advising   c. analyzing e.   supporting   g.   paraphrasing

b. judging d. questioning   f.   prompting

_____   1. "So what do you mean?"

_____   2. "You're mad at me for postponing the meeting?"

_____   3. "You're probably just more upset than usual because of the stress of exams."

_____   4. "What reason did she give for not attending?"

_____   5. "Well, that was good of him not to complain."

_____   6. "Have you tried praising her?"

_____   7. "Have you tried talking to him about it?"

_____   8. "Are you as excited as you sound about this big meet?"

_____   9. "Jim should not have said that to Amy after you asked him not to."

_____   10. "And then what happened?"

_____   11. "So why did you go to Ellie's in the first place?"

_____   12. "You really are good; they'll recognize that."

_____   13. "It's not fair for you to have to work nights."

_____   14. "Maybe you should give her a taste of her own medicine."

_____   15. "And so you feel like retaliating because you're hurt?"

_____   16. "Maybe you're a little insecure because of the divorce?"

_____ 17. "Like what?"

_____ 18. "What makes you think that he's cheating?"

_____ 19. "You've always pulled out those grades before—I know you can do it again."

_____ 20. "She's probably jealous so that's why she's doing that."

Choose the best listening response to each statement below.

21. Boss to employee: "Draft a letter that denies this request for a refund, but make it tactful."
     Identify the best paraphrasing response.

    a. "What do you want me to say?"
    b. "How can I say no tactfully?"
    c. "So I should explain nicely why we can't give a refund, right?"
    d. "In other words, you want me to give this customer the brush-off?"

22. Friend says, "How do they expect us to satisfy the course requirements when there aren't
     enough spaces in the classes we're supposed to take?" Identify the best questioning response.

    a. "What class do you need that you can't get into?"
    b. "You think that some of the courses are worthless—is that it?"
    c. "Sounds like you're sorry you chose this major."
    d. "Why don't you write a letter to the chairperson of the department?"

23. Friend says, "Why don't I meet you after class at the student union?" Identify the best
     questioning response.

    a. "So you want me to pick you up at the student union?"
    b. "You want me to pick you up *again*?"
    c. "What time do you think you'll be there?"
    d. "Why can't you drive yourself? Is your car broken again?"

24. Co-worker advises, "When you go in for a job interview, be sure and talk about the internship,
     your coursework, and your extracurricular activities. Don't expect them to ask you." Identify the
     best paraphrasing response.

    a. "You think they won't ask about those things?"
    b. "Won't that sound like bragging?"
    c. "Why should I talk about the internship?"
    d. "So you're saying not to be bashful about stressing my experience?"

25. Friend says, "I don't think it's right that they go out and recruit women when there are plenty of
     good men around." Identify the best supporting response.

    a. "I think you're job-hunting well in spite of the challenges."
    b. "You shouldn't let that bother you."
    c. "That's just the way life is."
    d. "I can see that you're angry. What makes you think women are being given an unfair
         advantage?"

For each of the statements below, identify which response is the most complete and accurate problem-solving reflection of the speaker's thoughts and feelings.

26. "Sometimes I think I'd like to drop out of school, but then I start to feel like a quitter."

    a. "Maybe it would be helpful to take a break. You can always come back, you know."
    b. "You're afraid that you might fail if you stay in school now, is that it?"
    c. "I can really relate to what you're saying. I feel awkward here myself sometimes."
    d. "So you'd feel ashamed of yourself if you quit now, even though you'd like to?"

27. "I don't want to go to the party. I won't know anyone there, and I'll wind up sitting by myself all night."

    a. "You're anxious about introducing yourself to people who don't know you?"
    b. "You never know; you could have a great time."
    c. "So you really don't want to go, eh?"
    d. "What makes you think it will be that way?"

28. "I get really nervous talking to my professor. I keep thinking that I sound stupid."

    a. "Talking to her is really a frightening experience?"
    b. "You're saying that you'd rather not approach her?"
    c. "You get the idea that she's evaluating you, so you feel inadequate?
    d. "You think that talking to her might affect your grade for the worse?"

29. "I don't know what to do about my kids. Their whining is driving me crazy."

    a. "Even though whining is natural, it's getting to you?"
    b. "Sometimes you lose patience when they complain?"
    c. "You're getting angry at them?"
    d. "Even the best parents get irritated sometimes."

30. "I just blew another test in that class. Why can't I do better?"

    a. "You probably need to study harder. You'll get it!"
    b. "You're feeling sorry for yourself because you can't pull a better grade?"
    c. "Where do you think the problem is?"
    d. "You're discouraged and frustrated because you don't know what you're doing wrong?"

CHAPTER 7 STUDY GUIDE ANSWERS

Crossword Puzzle

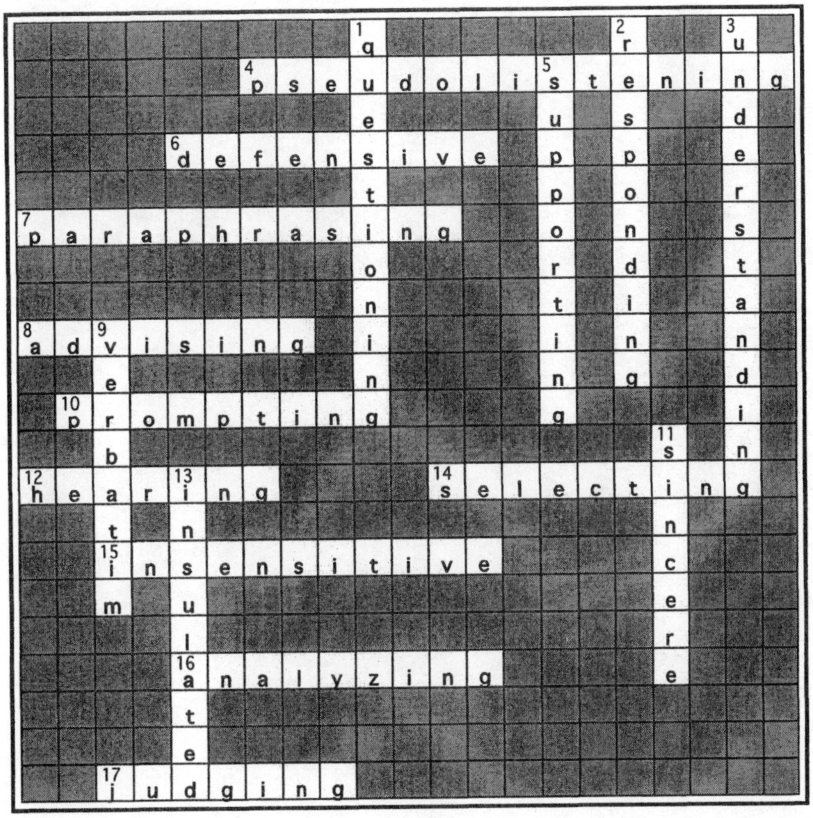

							1 a			2 r		3 u	
				4 p	s	e	u	d	o	5 l	i	s	t	e	n	i	n	g

(Crossword grid, across and down answers:)

- 4. pseudolistening
- 6. defensive
- 7. paraphrasing
- 8. advising
- 10. prompting
- 12. hearing
- 14. selecting
- 15. insensitive
- 16. analyzing
- 17. judging

Down answers visible in grid:
- 1. a...
- 2. responding
- 3. understanding
- 5. supporting
- 9. v...
- 11. sincerer
- 13. n...

True/False

| 1. T | 3. F | 5. T | 7. F | 9. T |
| 2. F | 4. T | 6. F | 8. F | 10. T |

Completion

1. conversational narcissist
2. sincere question
3. residual message
4. attending
5. counterfeit question
6. constructive criticism
7. hearing
8. understanding
9. remembering
10. agreement
11. selective
12. insulated

Multiple choice

1. f	7. a	13. b	19. e	25. a
2. g	8. g	14. a	20. c	26. d
3. c	9. b	15. g	21. c	27. a
4. d	10. f	16. c	22. a	28. c
5. b	11. d	17. f	23. c	29. b
6. a	12. e	18. d	24. d	30. d

Chapter Seven

CHAPTER EIGHT

COMMUNICATION AND RELATIONAL DYNAMICS

OUTLINE

Use this outline to take notes as you read the chapter in the text or as your instructor lectures in class.

I. **WHY WE FORM RELATIONSHIPS**
   A. **Attraction**
      1. Similarity and complementarity
      2. Reciprocal attraction
      3. Competence
      4. Disclosure
      5. Proximity
   B. **Intimacy**
      1. The dimensions of intimacy
         a. Physical
         b. Intellectual
         c. Emotional
         d. Shared activities
      2. Masculine and feminine intimacy styles
         a. Self-disclosure
         b. Shared activities
         c. Gender role
      3. Cultural influences on intimacy
         a. Historical
         b. Cultural
            1) Class/group
            2) Individualist/collectivist
      4. The limits of intimacy
   C. **Rewards - Social exchange theory**

II. **MODELS OF RELATIONAL DEVELOPMENT AND MAINTENANCE**
   A. **Developmental Models**
      1. Initiating
      2. Experimenting
      3. Intensifying
      4. Integrating
      5. Bonding
      6. Differentiating
      7. Circumscribing
      8. Stagnating
      9. Avoiding
      10. Terminating

   B. **Dialectical Perspectives**
      1. Dialectical tensions
         a. Connection vs. autonomy
         b. Predictability vs. novelty
         c. Openness vs. privacy
      2. Managing dialectical tensions
         a. Denial
         b. Disorientation
         c. Alternation
         d. Segmentation
         e. Balance
         f. Integration
         g. Recalibration
         h. Reaffirmation
   C. **Characteristics of Relational Development and Maintenance**
      1. Relationships are constantly changing
      2. Movement is always to a new place

III. **SELF-DISCLOSURE IN RELATIONSHIPS**
   A. **Definition**
      1. Deliberate
      2. Significant
      3. Not known by others
   B. **Characteristics of Self-Disclosure**
      1. Usually occurs in dyads
      2. Incremental
      3. Relatively scarce
      4. Best in context of positive relationships
   C. **Degrees of Self-Disclosure**
      1. Social penetration model: Breadth and depth
      2. Types: Clichés, facts, opinions, feelings
   D. **A Model of Self-Disclosure: Open, Hidden, Blind, Unknown**

E. **Reasons for Self-Disclosure**
1. Catharsis
2. Reciprocity
3. Self-clarification
4. Self-validation
5. Identity management
6. Relational maintenance and enhancement
7. Social control
8. Manipulation

F. **Guidelines for Self-Disclosure**
1. Consider the importance of the other person
2. Evaluate the risks involved
3. Make the disclosure relevant to the situation at hand
4. Make the amount and type of self-disclosure appropriate
5. Consider constructive effects
6. Make the disclosure clear and understandable
7. Reciprocate disclosure as appropriate

IV. **ALTERNATIVES TO SELF-DISCLOSURE**
A. **Lying**
1. Benevolent lies
2. Reasons for lying
a. Save face
b. Avoid tension/conflict
c. Guide social interaction
d. Expand/reduce relationships
e. Gain power
3. Effects of lies - threats to the relationship

B. **Equivocation**
1. Spares embarrassment
2. Saves face
3. Provides an alternative to lying

C. **Hinting**
1. Saves receiver from embarrassment
2. Saves sender from embarrassment

D. **The Ethics of Evasion**
1. Manage difficult situations
2. Honesty—avoid threat to relationship
3. Goes unchallenged
a. We expect others to lie.
b. The lie is mutually advantageous.
c. Lie helps us avoid embarrassment.
d. Lie helps us avoid confronting an unpleasant truth.
e. We have asked the other person to lie.

KEY TERMS

avoiding
benevolent lie
bonding
breadth
circumscribing
clichés
connection-autonomy dialectic
depth
dialectical tension
differentiating
experimenting
initiating

integrating
intensifying
intimacy
Johari Window
openness-privacy dialectic
predictability-novelty dialectic
relational maintenance
self-disclosure
social penetration
stagnating
terminating

ACTIVITIES

8.1 DISCOVERING DIALECTICS

◆ **Activity Type: Invitation to Insight**

Purpose

To identify and describe behaviors that contribute to dialectical tensions in relationships.

Instructions

1. Identify the dialectical tensions operating in the situations below, taking time to explain the conflicting feelings and thoughts in each.
2. Identify one or more of the eight strategies for managing dialectical tensions (denial, disorientation, selection, alternation, segmentation, moderation, reframing and reaffirmation) that you believe would be most beneficial to the relationship, and explain how the relationship would deal with the dialectical tension under these circumstances.
3. Describe dialectical tensions at work in your own relationships and label and explain the strategies that you use to deal with them.

SITUATION	DIALECTICAL TENSION	STRATEGY FOR MANAGING
Example: *Sandra, nineteen, and her mother, Tracy, have become good friends over the past few years. Sandra now has a serious boyfriend and spends less time talking to her mother.*	*The open-privacy dialectic is probably at work here. Sandra and Tracy continue to share the intimacy of their mother-daughter relationship, but privacy needs about the boyfriend probably keep them at more distance.*	*Sandra and Tracy are likely to use the segmentation strategy, in which they maintain openness about many areas but keep certain areas of the boyfriend relationship "off limits."*
1. Daryl is new to the software firm where Steve has been for five years. Daryl has asked Steve to play golf this weekend. Steve is uncomfortable about mixing business and pleasure, but still wants to have a good working relationship with Daryl.		
2. Nesto and Gina have been dating for six months. They continue to enjoy one another's company, but each has begun to notice annoying little habits that the other one has.		

SITUATION	DIALECTICAL TENSION	STRATEGY FOR MANAGING
3. Jenner and A. J. are siblings who have always relied on one another completely. Jenner appreciates A. J.'s dependability, but wishes their relationship wasn't so boring.		
4. Eugenia and Shane have worked at the same business for twenty years. They have collaborated on a number of projects. They've tried to get together socially, but Eugenia's husband and Shane's wife don't seem to get along.		
5. Christina and Nicole are roommates. Christina wants them to share everything, but Nicole is not proud of a few things she's done and doesn't want to face her friend's judgment.		
6. Richard and Matt have been best friends for over ten years. Richard met a woman over a year ago and married her last month. Both Richard and Matt are trying to work out their "new" relationship.		
7. Your example:		
8. Your example:		

8.2 RELATIONAL STAGES

❖ Activity Type: Skill Builder

Purposes

1. To identify typical relational behaviors.
2. To identify stages of relational development that the behaviors typify.

Instructions

1. Discuss the various situations listed below.
2. List behaviors that relational partners are likely to exhibit (e.g., verbal and nonverbal behaviors, equivocation, lies, disclosure).
3. Determine the function that response serves in the relationship (e.g., advancing or reducing intimacy, maintaining).
4. Identify the relational stage(s) that may these behaviors illustrate (e.g., initiating, experimenting, intensifying, integrating, bonding, differentiating, circumscribing, avoiding, stagnating, terminating).
5. Record relational situations of your own in the same manner.

Example

Two friends are discussing the effects of divorce in their families.

Type(s) of responses likely *Self-disclosure is likely to occur in this situation. Because they have similar experiences, the likelihood of reciprocity of self-disclosure is high. It will probably come from the highest levels of self-disclosure, feelings, but might also include a number of facts.*

Function in relationship *The self-disclosure functions to maintain the relationship, to increase intellectual and emotional intimacy, and to advance the stage of the relationship.*

Relational stage illustrated *This type of self-disclosure would most likely occur in an intensifying stage of a relationship, where the friends have gone beyond the small talk of experimenting and are beginning to develop more trust, more depth rather than breadth of self-disclosure, and where secrets are told and favors given.*

1. Two friends are telling one another about using / refusing drugs.

   Behaviors that are likely _____

   _____

   Function in relationship _____

   Relational stage illustrated _____

2. Two classmates are comparing the results of their first exam.

   Behaviors that are likely _____

   _____

   Function in relationship _____

   Relational stage illustrated _____

3. A boyfriend and girlfriend are telling one another about their past romantic involvements.

Behaviors that are likely _____

_____

Function in relationship _____

Relational stage illustrated _____

_____

4. Two long-term friends are discussing their worries and feelings of responsibility regarding their parents' advancing age.

Behaviors that are likely _____

_____

Function in relationship _____

Relational stage illustrated _____

_____

5. Parents ask their twenty-year-old about his or her weekend.

Behaviors that are likely _____

_____

Function in relationship _____

Relational stage illustrated _____

6. A divorced couple meets briefly to discuss education and vacation plans for their children.

Behaviors that are likely _____

_____

Function in relationship _____

Relational stage illustrated _____

_____

7. A man and woman who dated for six months during college find themselves working for the same company.

Behaviors that are likely _____

_____

Function in relationship _____

Relational stage illustrated _____

_____

8. A manager and employee have agreed to sit down and talk about the problems they are experiencing with each other.

Behaviors that are likely _____

_____

Function in relationship _____

Relational stage illustrated _____

_____

9. Your example: _____

Behaviors that are likely _____

_____

Function in relationship _____

Relational stage illustrated _____

_____

10. Your example: _____

Behaviors that are likely _____

_____

Function in relationship _____

Relational stage illustrated _____

8.3 BREADTH AND DEPTH OF RELATIONSHIPS

◆ Activity Type: Invitation to Insight

Purposes

1. To help you understand the breadth and depth of a relationship that is important to you.
2. To help you decide if you are satisfied with the breadth and depth of that relationship, and possibly to modify it.

Instructions

1. Use the form below to make a social penetration model for a significant relationship you have, indicating the depth and breadth of various areas. See Figure 8.4 and 8.5 in Chapter 8 of *Looking Out/Looking In* for an example of the social penetration model.
2. Answer the questions at the end of the exercise.

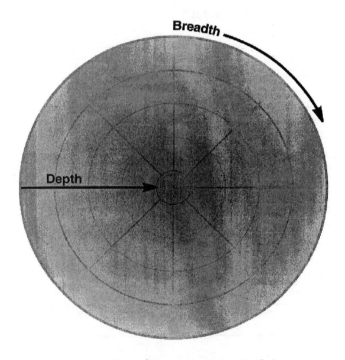

FIGURE 8-5   **Social Penetration Model**

Significant relationship described: _____

Conclusions

How deep or shallow is your relationship with this person?

_____

_____

Does the depth vary from one area (breadth) to another? In what way?

_____

_____

_____

Are you satisfied with the depth and breadth of this relationship?

_____

_____

_____

What could you do to change the relationship?

_____

_____

_____

_____

_____

_____

_____

_____

8.4 REASONS FOR NONDISCLOSURE

◆ **Activity Type: Invitation to Insight**

Purpose

To give you an idea of the reasons you do not disclose and the rationality of these reasons.

Instructions

1. Choose a particular individual about whom you want to analyze your self-disclosing behavior.
2. In the column to the left of each item, indicate the extent to which you use each reason to avoid disclosing.
   5 = almost always   2 = rarely
   4 = often   1 = never
   3 = sometimes
3. In the column to the right of each item, indicate how reasonable and realistic the reason is.
   5 = totally realistic
   4 = mostly realistic
   3 = partly realistic, partly unrealistic
   2 = mostly unrealistic
   1 = totally unrealistic

How Frequently Do You Use the Reason?			How Realistic and Rational Is the Reason?
_____	1.	I can't find the opportunity to self-disclose with this person.	_____
_____	2.	If I disclose I might hurt the other person.	_____
_____	3.	If I disclose I might be evaluating or judging the person.	_____
_____	4.	I can't think of topics that I would disclose.	_____
_____	5.	Self-disclosure would give information that might be used against me at some time.	_____
_____	6.	If I disclose it might cause me to make personal changes.	_____
_____	7.	Self-disclosure might threaten relationships I have with people other than the close acquaintance to whom I disclose.	_____
_____	8.	Self-disclosure is a sign of weakness.	_____
_____	9.	If I disclose I might lose control over the other person.	_____
_____	10.	If I disclose I might discover I am less than I wish to be.	_____

*Based on a survey developed by Lawrence B. Rosenfeld, "Self-Disclosure Avoidance: Why Am I Afraid to Tell You Who I Am?" *Communication Monographs* 46 (1979): 63–74.

**How Frequently
Do You Use
the Reason?**

**How Realistic
and Rational
Is the Reason?**

_____	11. If I disclose I might project an image I do not want to project.	_____
_____	12. If I disclose the other person might not understand what I was saying.	_____
_____	13. If I disclose the other person might evaluate me negatively.	_____
_____	14. Self-disclosure is a sign of some emotional disturbance.	_____
_____	15. Self-disclosure might hurt our relationship.	_____
_____	16. I am afraid that self-disclosure might lead to an intimate relationship with the other person.	_____
_____	17. Self-disclosure might threaten my physical safety.	_____
_____	18. If I disclose I might give information that makes me appear inconsistent.	_____
_____	19. Any other reasons: _____	_____

What does this personal survey tell you about your thoughts and feelings about self-disclosure with this person?

_____

_____

_____

Do you think your level of self-disclosure is appropriate or inappropriate with this person? Why?

_____

_____

8.5 DEGREES OF SELF-DISCLOSURE

◆ Activity Type: Invitation to Insight

Purposes

1. To demonstrate that self-disclosure can operate on a variety of levels, some quite intimate and others less revealing.
2. To give you practice in applying various types of self-disclosure to personal situations.

Instructions

For each of the following topics, write two statements for each level of self-disclosure. (See Chapter 8 of *Looking Out/Looking In* for descriptions of each level.)

Example

Topic: School
1. Clichés
   a. *Finals are no fun!*
   b. *Textbooks sure are expensive!*
2. Facts
   a. *I'm a psychology major at the university.*
   b. *I'm getting a teaching certificate so I'll be able to teach social studies.*
3. Opinions
   a. *I believe in affirmative action but I don't think there should be quotas for women and minorities.*
   b. *I don't think instructors should count attendance as part of a person's grade.*
4. Feelings
   a. *I feel scared when I think about the future. I'm almost finished with four years of college, and I'm still confused about what to do with my life.*
   b. *I get angry when Professor Autel doesn't prepare adequately for our class.*

Topic: My family

1. Clichés

   a. _____

   b. _____

2. Facts

   a. _____

   b. _____

3. Opinions

   a. _____

   b. _____

4. Feelings

   a. _____

   b. _____

Topic: My career plans

1. Clichés

   a. _____

   b. _____

2. Facts

   a. _____

   b. _____

3. Opinions

   a. _____

   b. _____

4. Feelings

   a. _____

   b. _____

Topic: My friendships

1. Clichés

   a. _____

   b. _____

2. Facts

   a. _____

   b. _____

3. Opinions

   a. _____

   b. _____

4. Feelings

   a. _____

   b. _____

Topic: Sports

1. Clichés

   a. _____

   b. _____

2. Facts

   a. _____

   b. _____

3. Opinions

   a. _____

   b. _____

4. Feelings

   a. _____

   b. _____

8.6 DISCLOSURE AND ALTERNATIVES

❖ Activity Type: Skill Builder

Purposes

1. To generate responses to relational situations.
2. To evaluate the effectiveness and ethics of each situation.

Instructions

1. For each situations described below, record responses for the types listed.
2. Evaluate the effectiveness and ethics of your responses.
3. Describe a disclosure situation of your own in the same manner.

Example

Your friend asks you if you had a good time when you went out with his cousin last night.
Self-disclosure *I didn't have a great time, but then we were just getting to know one another. I don't think that we had much in common.*
Partial disclosure *I enjoyed the movie.*
Benevolent lie or lie *Your cousin was a lot of fun and the movie was great.*
Hinting or equivocation *First dates are really times of discovery, aren't they?*
Which response is most effective/which most ethical? *I think the benevolent lie was most effective. While I wasn't exactly truthful with my friend, I just don't want to tell him how boring I think his cousin is. I think it is better to just be nice to him and his cousin. Then both of them can save face, too.*

1. After your romantic partner has a bad week at work, his/her boss asks you how he/she is feeling about the company.

   Self-disclosure_____

   Partial disclosure _____

   Benevolent lie or lie _____

   Hinting or equivocation _____

   Which responses are most effective/which most ethical?_____

   _____

   _____

2. You are applying to rent an apartment that prohibits animals. You have a cat.

   Self-disclosure_____

   Partial disclosure _____

   Benevolent lie or lie _____

   Hinting or equivocation _____

   Which responses are most effective/which most ethical?_____

_____

_____

3. Your sibling accuses you of telling family secrets to a mutual friend.

    Self-disclosure_____

    Partial disclosure _____

    Benevolent lie or lie _____

    Hinting or equivocation _____

    Which responses are most effective/which most ethical?_____

    _____

    _____

4. Your roommates ask what you think of the bright posters they've just put up around the living room.

    Self-disclosure_____

    Partial disclosure _____

    Benevolent lie or lie _____

    Hinting or equivocation _____

    Which responses are most effective/which most ethical?_____

    _____

    _____

5. Your romantic partner asks how many other people you've really loved before you met him or her.

    Self-disclosure_____

    Partial disclosure _____

    Benevolent lie or lie _____

    Hinting or equivocation _____

    Which responses are most effective/which most ethical?_____

    _____

    _____

6. Your very opinionated father asks what you think of the people running for political office.

   Self-disclosure_____

   Partial disclosure _____

   Benevolent lie or lie _____

   Hinting or equivocation _____

   Which responses are most effective/which most ethical?_____

   _____

   _____

7. Your boss at work wants to know what your plans for the future are; you're looking around.

   Self-disclosure_____

   Partial disclosure _____

   Benevolent lie or lie _____

   Hinting or equivocation _____

   Which responses are most effective/which most ethical?_____

   _____

   _____

8. Your mother asks you about what your brother/sister has been up to lately.

   Self-disclosure_____

   Partial disclosure _____

   Benevolent lie or lie _____

   Hinting or equivocation _____

   Which responses are most effective/which most ethical?_____

   _____

   _____

9. Your example: _____

   Self-disclosure_____

   Partial disclosure _____

   Benevolent lie or lie _____

Hinting or equivocation _____

Which responses are most effective/which most ethical? _____

_____

8.7 MEDIATED MESSAGES – RELATIONAL DYNAMICS

❖ **Activity Type: Group Discussion**

Purpose

To analyze relational dynamics in mediated contexts.

Instructions

Discuss each of the questions below in your group. Prepare written answers for your instructor, or be prepared to contribute to a large group discussion, comparing your experiences with those of others in your class.

1. Identify how mediated forms of communication (e.g. instant messaging/chat, e-mail) can help us form relationships (i.e., build attraction, create intimacy). Do mediated forms of communication make it easier to form relationships or are we more isolated relationally because of mediated communication? For a brief background article, use your InfoTrac connection to read *Escaping or connecting? Characteristics of youth who form close online relationships* by Sue Headley (*Youth Studies Australia*, March 2003, v22, p. 60(1)).

_____

_____

_____

_____

_____

2. When people are physically separated, maintaining relationships is difficult. Discuss how mediated forms of communication might be employed effectively in these cases.

_____

_____

_____

_____

_____

3. Describe how self-disclosure might occur differently in mediated contexts (letters, e-mail, telephone, instant messaging/chat, online courses) than in face-to-face communication. Can satisfying relationships be maintained without face-to-face communication?

_____

_____

_____

4. Discuss how physical, intellectual and emotional intimacy (and even shared activities) can be fostered using mediated forms of communication.

_____

_____

_____

_____

_____

8.8 YOUR CALL – RELATIONAL DYNAMICS

❖ **Activity Type: Group Discussion**

Purpose

To analyze the role of self-disclosure in a relationship.

Instructions

Use the case below and the discussion questions that follow to discuss the variety of communication issues involved in effective communication. Make notes on this page, add other pages on your own, or prepare a group report/analysis based on your discussion. Add your own experiences to individualize the analysis to make it **Your Call**.

Case

Leilani and Malcolm dated one another exclusively for three years. They broke up for six months, and now are back together and talking about getting married. While they were broken up, Leilani became intimate with a casual friend of Malcolm's for a brief time before she realized that she really loved only Malcolm. During this same time period, Malcolm dated around; he was attracted to a number of women, but he did not get serious about any one. Malcolm has now told Leilani that he believes they should tell one another everything about the time they were apart.

1. Do you think full self-disclosure is important in this relationship? Why or why not?

   _____

   _____

   _____

   _____

2. Use other relationships (your own and others) to evaluate how important full self-disclosure is to committed relationships. Cite times when full disclosure may be more harmful than helpful?

   _____

   _____

   _____

   _____

3. Evaluate the alternatives to self-disclosure in this situation. Explain how lies, benevolent lies, partial disclosure, equivocation or hinting might be more effective than full disclosure?

   _____

   _____

   _____

   _____

4. Read http://mentalhelp.net/psyhelp/chap13/chap13i.htm for advice about self-disclosure. Compare it to the text's advice about self-disclosure and then evaluate how much Leilani and Malcolm should disclose to each other about the six months they were apart.

_____

_____

_____

_____

8.9 DEAR PROFESSOR – RELATIONAL RESPONSES

◆❖ Activity Type: Invitation to Insight/Group Discussion

Purposes

1. To examine communication challenges addressed by this chapter.
2. To demonstrate your ability to analyze communication challenges using the concepts in this chapter.

Instructions

1. Read the Dear Professor letter and response below.
2. Discuss ProfMary's response. Would you add anything or give a different response?
3. Read the second letter. Construct an answer to it, <u>using terms and concepts from this chapter.</u> <u>Underline or boldface the terms and concepts you apply here.</u>
4. If class structure permits, share your letters and answers with other members of the class.

Part A - The letter

Dear Professor,
Sometimes I feel neglected by my mom. She seldom calls me since I've been away at college. She's so busy doing her yoga and with my younger brother that she always sounds rushed when I call. I want to let her know that I want her to make more of an effort to call me and visit me without sounding needy or like I can't take care of myself. I have my own life away from her, but I want to maintain the close relationship we've always had. **Tylor**

The response

Dear Tylor,
*Since you've always had a close relationship with your mom, it is unlikely that this present behavior is a threat. Perhaps the kinds of **intimacy** you've shared are different now that you don't live in the same place. The **physical intimacy** of living together and the **emotional intimacy** of sharing your lives daily are not there. You want something to replace that.*
*Your mom may be consciously trying to recognize your independence by giving you more **autonomy** now that you're away at college. You probably want that to some extent, but want to maintain the **connectedness** with her as well. This is a normal relational strain called a **dialectic**. You can manage it directly by addressing it with your mother, or you can decide to accept the new situation as a part of the growth of your new life, or you can try to **recalibrate** what's comfortable for both of you.*
Do tell your mom that you want to maintain the closeness you've had with her, even if that closeness gets redefined. Give her some examples of what you would like to happen (e.g., come to visit you on a special weekend, call you every Sunday) and then ask her if she has time for any of them.

In hopes for your relational satisfaction,   ***ProfMary***

Part B - The letter

Dear Professor,

What are some positive ways to deal with the ending of a romantic relationship? I've moved, and we tried to keep it going long-distance, but that's not working. How do I redefine the relationship so that we remain friends but not be romantically involved? **Griffin**

Your response

Dear Griffin,

_____

_____

_____

_____

_____

_____

_____

_____

_____

_____

_____

_____

Study Guide

CHECK YOUR UNDERSTANDING

Crossword puzzle

ACROSS

2. the second level of disclosure that discloses information about the self
3. first dimension of self-disclosure involving the range of subjects being discussed
7. a state of personal sharing arising from physical, intellectual, or emotional contact
9. the process of deliberately revealing information about oneself that is significant and that would not normally be known by others is self-_____
11. a semi-economic social _____ theory of relationships that suggests we often seek out people who can give us rewards that are greater than or equal to the costs we encounter in dealing with them
15. confirmation of a belief you hold about yourself is self-_____

16. a social _____ model that describes relationships in terms of their breadth and depth
17. a model of relationships that describes broad phases of "coming together" and "coming apart"

DOWN

1. disclosing information in an attempt to "get it off your chest"
4. using ambiguous language that has two or more equally plausible meanings
5. a dimension of self-disclosure involving a shift from relatively nonrevealing messages to more personal ones
6. giving subtle clues to get a desired response from others without direct stating it

8. an act of self-disclosure calculated in advance to achieve a desired result

10. a motivation for self-disclosing based on the research evidence that individuals disclosing information about themselves encourage others to self-disclose in return

12. a motivation for self-disclosing based on creating relational success by increasing honesty and depth of sharing

13. speech that focuses on building beginning relationships, usually focusing on similarities with the other person is _____ talk

14. a model that describes the relationship between self-disclosure and self-awareness is the _____ Window

True/False

Mark the statements below as true or false. Correct statements that are false on the lines below to create a true statement.

_____ 1. Intimacy is definitely rewarding, so maximizing intimacy is the best way of relating to others.

_____ 2. An obsession with intimacy can actually lead to less satisfying relationships.

_____ 3. Research shows that male-male relationships involve less disclosure than male-female or female-female relationships.

_____ 4. Women are better at developing and maintaining intimate relationships than men.

_____ 5. Germans and Japanese are more disclosing than members of any culture studied.

_____

_____

_____

_____

_____ 6. The struggle to achieve important, but seemingly incompatible goals in relationships, results in the creation of dialectical tension.

_____

_____

_____

_____

_____ 7. The struggle between independence and dependence in a relationship is called the openness-privacy dialectic.

_____

_____

_____

_____

_____ 8. Your strongest relationships will be stable for long periods of time.

_____

_____

_____

_____

_____ 9. Research indicates that partners in intimate relationships engage in high levels of self-disclosure frequently.

_____

_____

_____

_____

_____ 10. People justify over half of their lies as ways to avoid embarrassment for themselves or others.

_____

_____

_____

_____

_____ 11. Relational partners go through evolving cycles in which they can repeat a relational stage at a new level.

_____

_____

_____

_____

_____ 12. Differences strengthen a relationship when they are complementary.

_____

_____

_____

_____

_____ 13. In a casual relationship, the depth of self-disclosure may be great, but not the breadth.

_____

_____

_____

_____

_____ 14. Biological sex is the most significant influence on a man's expression of intimacy.

_____

_____

_____

_____

_____ 15. In some collectivistic cultures, there is a great difference between the way people communicate with members of their "in-groups" and with their "out-groups."

_____

_____

_____

_____

Completion

Fill in the blanks below with the correct terms chosen from the list below.

| open | hidden | blind | unknown | intellectual |
| physical | emotional | integration | hinting | attraction |

1. _____ is the type of intimacy that comes from an exchange of important ideas.

2. _____ is the type of intimacy that comes from touching, struggling, or sex.

3. _____ is the type of intimacy that comes from exchanging important feelings.

4. _____ is an explanation for what makes us want to develop personal relationships with some people and not with others.

5. _____ is an acceptance of opposing dialectical tensions without trying to diminish them.

6. _____ is a frame of the Johari Window that consists of information that you know about yourself but aren't willing to reveal to others.

7. _____ is a frame of the Johari Window that consists of information of which neither you nor the other person is aware.

8. _____ is a frame of the Johari Window that consists of information of which both you and the other person are aware.

9. _____ is a frame of the Johari Window that consists of information of which you are unaware but the other person in the relationship knows.

10. _____ is an alternative to self-disclosure in which the person gives only a clue to the direct meaning of the response.

11. _____ is a type of lie that is intended to help, not harm others.

12. _____ is a tension that arises when two incompatible goals exist in a relationship.

Multiple Choice

Place the letter of the developmental stage of the intimate relationship on the line before its example found below.

a. initiating   f. differentiating
b. experimenting   g. circumscribing
c. intensifying   h. stagnating
d. integrating   i. avoiding
e. bonding   j. terminating

_____ 1. A public ritual marks this stage.

_____ 2. First glances and "sizing up" each other typifies this stage.

_____ 3. Called the "we" stage, this stage involves increasing self-disclosure.

_____ 4. Lots of "small talk" typifies this stage.

_____ 5. This stage involves much focus on individual rather than dyadic interests.

_____ 6. There's very little growth or experimentation in this stage.

_____ 7. This stage involves much behavior that talks around the relational issues because the partners expect bad feelings.

_____ 8. The partners' social circles merge at this stage and they make purchases or commitments together.

_____ 9. No attempts are made to contact the other at this stage.

_____ 10. The relationship is redefined or dissolved at this stage.

_____ 11. A marriage ceremony would be typical here.

_____ 12. Roommates who make sure they are never in the same room and who are tolerating one another only until the lease is up might be at this stage.

_____ 13. A couple who avoids talking about future commitment because they are afraid of how the discussion will go is probably at this state.

_____ 14. This stage represents most communication at a social gathering where people are just getting to know one another.

_____ 15. In this stage, people spend an increasing amount of time together, asking for support from one another and doing favors for one another.

CHAPTER 8 STUDY GUIDE ANSWERS

Crossword puzzle

```
                                              ¹c
                                          ²f  a  c  t  s
                                              t
                                              h
 ³b  r  e  a  d  t  h                         a
     a     e     ⁷i  n  t  ⁸i  m  a  c  y     r
     u     p     n         a                  s
     i     t     t         n                  i
     v     h     i     ⁹d  i  s  c  l  o  s  u  r  e
¹⁰r  o     i     n         p
¹¹e  x  c  h  a  n  g  e  ¹²e         ¹³s
     c     a     n         u          m       ¹⁴J
     i     t     ¹⁵h  a  l  i  d  a  t  i  o  n
     p     i     a         t          l       h
     r     n     n         i          l       a
     o     g     c         o          s       r
     c           e         n                  i
     i           m
     t        ¹⁶p  e  n  e  t  r  a  t  i  o  n
     y           n
              ¹⁷s  t  a  i  r  c  a  s  e
```

True/False

1. F	4. F	7. F	10. T	13. F
2. T	5. F	8. T	11. T	14. F
3. T	6. T	9. F	12. T	15. T

Completion

1. intellectual	5. integration	9. blind
2. physical	6. hidden	10. hinting
3. emotional	7. unknown	11. benevolent
4. attraction variable	8. open	12. dialectical

Multiple choice

1. e	4. b	7. g	10. j	13. g
2. a	5. f	8. d	11. e	14. b
3. c	6. h	9. i	12. i	15. c

IMPROVING COMMUNICATION CLIMATES

OUTLINE

Use this outline to take notes as you read the chapter in the text and/or as your instructor lectures in class.

I. **COMMUNICATION CLIMATE: THE KEY TO POSITIVE RELATIONSHIPS**
   A. **Types of Confirming Messages**
      1. Recognition
      2. Acknowledgement
      3. Endorsement
   B. **Disconfirming Messages**
      1. Verbal abuse
      2. Generalized complaining
      3. Impervious responses
      4. Interrupting
      5. Irrelevant responses
      6. Tangential responses
      7. Impersonal responses
      8. Ambiguous responses
      9. Incongruous responses
   C. **How Communication Climates Develop**
      1. Escalatory conflict spirals
      2. De-escalatory conflict spirals

II. **DEFENSIVENESS: CAUSES AND REMEDIES**
   A. **Causes: Face-Threatening Acts**
   B. **Types of Defensive Reactions**
      1. Attacking the critic
         a. Verbal aggression
         b. Sarcasm
      2. Distorting critical information
         a. Rationalization
         b. Compensation
         c. Regression
      3. Avoiding dissonant information
         a. Physical avoidance
         b. Repression
         c. Apathy
         d. Displacement

C. **Preventing Defensiveness in Others**
   1. Evaluation versus description
   2. Control versus problem orientation
   3. Strategy versus spontaneity
   4. Neutrality versus empathy
   5. Superiority versus equality
   6. Certainty versus provisionalism

III. **SAVING FACE: THE CLEAR MESSAGE FORMAT**
   A. **Behavior**
   B. **Interpretation**
      1. Your past experience
      2. Your assumptions
      3. Your expectations
      4. Your knowledge
      5. Your current mood
   C. **Feeling**
   D. **Consequence**
      1. What happens to you, the speaker
      2. What happens to the person you're addressing
      3. What happens to others
   E. **Intention**
      1. Where you stand on an issue
      2. Requests of others
      3. Descriptions of how you plan to act in the future
   F. **Using the Clear Message Format**
      1. May be delivered in mixed order
      2. Word to suit your personal style
      3. Combine elements when appropriate
      4. Take your time delivering the message

IV. RESPONDING NONDEFENSIVELY TO CRITICISM
A. Seek more information
1. Ask for specifics
2. Guess about specifics
3. Paraphrase the speaker's ideas
4. Ask what the critic wants
5. Ask what else is wrong

B. Agree with the critic
1. Agree with the facts
2. Agree with the critic's perception

KEY TERMS

ambiguous response
apathy
behavioral description
certainty
cognitive dissonance
communication climate
compensation
confirming communication
consequence statement
controlling communication
de-escalatory conflict spiral
defense mechanism
defensiveness
description
disconfirming communication
displacement
empathy
equality
escalatory conflict spiral
evaluation
face-threatening act
feeling statement
Gibb categories

impersonal response
impervious response
incongruous response
intention statement
interpretation statement
interrupting response
irrelevant response
neutrality
physical avoidance
problem orientation
provisionalism
rationalization
regression
repression
sarcasm
spiral
spontaneity
strategy
superiority
tangential response
verbal abuse
verbal aggression

ACTIVITIES

9.1 UNDERSTANDING DEFENSIVE RESPONSES

◆ **Activity Type: Invitation to Insight**

Purpose

To identify typical defensive responses.

Instructions

1. Identify the person or people who would be most likely to deliver each of the following critical messages to you. If you are unlikely to hear one or more of the following messages, substitute a defensiveness-arousing topic of your own.
2. For each situation, describe
    a. the person likely to deliver the message.
    b. the typical content of the message.
    c. the general type of response(s) you make: attacking, distorting, or avoiding.
    d. your typical verbal response(s).
    e. your typical nonverbal response(s).
    f. the part of your presenting self being defended.
    g. the probable consequences of these response(s).

Example

A negative comment about your use of time.
Person likely to deliver this message *my parents*
Typical content of the message *wasting my time watching TV instead of studying*
General type(s) of response *attacking, distorting*
Your typical verbal response(s) *"Get off my back! I work hard! I need time to relax." "I'll study later; I've got plenty of time."*
Your typical nonverbal response(s) *harsh tone of voice, sullen silence for an hour or two*
Part of presenting self being defended *good student, not lazy*
Probable consequences of your response(s) *uncomfortable silence, more criticism from parents in the future*

1. Negative comment about your appearance.

    Person likely to deliver this message _____

    Typical content of the message _____

    _____

    General type(s) of response _____

    Your typical verbal response(s) _____

    _____

    Your typical nonverbal response(s) _____

_____

Part(s) of presenting self being defended _____

Probable consequences of your response(s) _____

_____

_____

2. Criticism about your choice of friends.

   Person likely to deliver this message _____

   Typical content of the message _____

   _____

   General type(s) of response _____

   Your typical verbal response(s) _____

   _____

   Your typical nonverbal response(s) _____

   _____

   Part(s) of presenting self being defended _____

   Probable consequences of your response(s) _____

   _____

   _____

3. Criticism of a job you've just completed.

   Person likely to deliver this message _____

   Typical content of the message _____

   _____

   General type(s) of response _____

   Your typical verbal response(s) _____

   _____

   Your typical nonverbal response(s) _____

_____

Part(s) of presenting self being defended _____

Probable consequences of your response(s) _____

_____

_____

4. Criticism of your schoolwork.

   Person likely to deliver this message _____

   Typical content of the message _____

   _____

   General type(s) of response _____

   Your typical verbal response(s) _____

   _____

   Your typical nonverbal response(s) _____

   _____

   Part(s) of presenting self being defended _____

   Probable consequences of your response(s) _____

   _____

   _____

5. Criticism of your diet or eating habits.

   Person likely to deliver this message _____

   Typical content of the message _____

   _____

   General type(s) of response _____

   Your typical verbal response(s) _____

   _____

   Your typical nonverbal response(s) _____

   _____

Part(s) of presenting self being defended _____

Probable consequences of your response(s) _____

_____

_____

6. A negative comment about your exercise (or lack of it).

Person likely to deliver this message _____

Typical content of the message _____

_____

General type(s) of response _____

Your typical verbal response(s) _____

_____

Your typical nonverbal response(s) _____

_____

Part(s) of presenting self being defended _____

Probable consequences of your response(s) _____

_____

_____

9.2 DEFENSIVE AND SUPPORTIVE LANGUAGE

◆❖ Activity Type: Skill Builder

Purpose

To recognize the difference between the Gibb categories of defensive and supportive language.

Instructions

1. For each of the situations below, write one defense-arousing statement and one supportive statement.
2. Label the Gibb category of language that each statement represents (evaluation, description, control, problem-orientation, strategy, spontaneity, neutrality, empathy, superiority, equality, certainty, or provisionalism).

Example

A neighbor's late-night stereo music playing is disrupting your sleep.
Defense-arousing statement *Why don't you show a little consideration and turn that damn thing down? If I hear any more noise I'm going to call the police!*
Type(s) of defensive language *evaluation, control*
Supportive statement *When I hear your stereo music late at night I can't sleep, which leaves me more and more tired. I'd like to figure out some way you can listen and I can sleep.*
Type(s) of supportive language *description, problem orientation*

1. You're an adult child who moves back in with your parents. They say they expect you to follow the "rules of the house."

   Defense-arousing statement _____

   _____

   Type(s) of defensive language _____

   Supportive statement _____

   _____

   Type(s) of supportive language _____

2. Your roommate tells you you're trying to be "somebody you're not."

   Defense-arousing statement _____

   _____

   Type(s) of defensive language _____

   Supportive statement _____

   _____

   Type(s) of supportive language _____

3. A friend asks you what you see in your new romantic partner.

Defense-arousing statement _____

_____

Type(s) of defensive language _____

Supportive statement_____

_____

Type(s) of supportive language _____

4. Your boss says, "You call that finished?"

Defense-arousing statement _____

_____

Type(s) of defensive language _____

Supportive statement_____

_____

Type(s) of supportive language _____

5. Your friend buys the same thing you did after you bragged about the deal you got.

Defense-arousing statement _____

_____

Type(s) of defensive language _____

Supportive statement_____

_____

Type(s) of supportive language _____

6. On many occasions a friend drops by your place without calling first. Since you often have other plans, this behavior puts you in an uncomfortable position.

Defense-arousing statement _____

_____

Type(s) of defensive language _____

Supportive statement_____

_____

Class _____   Name _____

Type(s) of supportive language _____

7. Your roommate says, "You left the lights on *again*."

   Defense-arousing statement _____

   _____

   Type(s) of defensive language _____

   Supportive statement _____

   _____

   Type(s) of supportive language _____

8. Your parent praises your sibling for something without mentioning you.

   Defense-arousing statement _____

   _____

   Type(s) of defensive language _____

   Supportive statement _____

   _____

   Type(s) of supportive language _____

9. Your situation:_____

   Defense-arousing statement _____

   _____

   Type(s) of defensive language _____

   Supportive statement _____

   _____

   Type(s) of supportive language _____

9.3 WRITING CLEAR MESSAGES

◆❖ Activity Type: Skill Builder

Purpose

To turn unclear messages into clear ones.

Instructions

Imagine a situation in which you might have said each of the statements below. Rewrite the messages in the clear message format, being sure to include each of the five elements described in your text.

Example

Unclear message: "It's awful when you can't trust a friend."

Clear message:

Lena, when I gave you the keys to my house so you could borrow those clothes.	(behavior)
I figured you'd know to lock up again when you left.	(interpretation)
I was worried and scared.	(feeling)
Because I found the door unlocked and thought there was a break-in.	(consequence)
I want to know if you left the house open and, let you know how upset I am.	(intention)

1. "Blast it, Robin! Get off my back."

    _____ (behavior)

    _____ (interpretation)

    _____ (feeling)

    _____ (consequence)

    _____ (intention)

2. "I wish you'd pay more attention to me."

    _____ (behavior)

    _____ (interpretation)

    _____ (feeling)

    _____ (consequence)

    _____ (intention)

3. "You've sure been thoughtful lately."

_____ (behavior)

_____ (interpretation)

_____ (feeling)

_____ (consequence)

_____ (intention)

4. "Nobody's perfect!"

_____ (behavior)

_____ (interpretation)

_____ (feeling)

_____ (consequence)

_____ (intention)

5. "Matt, you're such a slob!"

_____ (behavior)

_____ (interpretation)

_____ (feeling)

_____ (consequence)

_____ (intention)

6. "Let's just forget it; with all the screaming, I get flustered."

_____ (behavior)

_____ (interpretation)

_____ (feeling)

_____ (consequence)

_____ (intention)

7. "I really shouldn't eat any of that cake you baked."

_____ (behavior)

_____ (interpretation)

_____ (feeling)

_____ (consequence)

_____ (intention)

Now list three significant messages that you could send to important people in your life: complaints, requests, or expressions of appreciation. Write them in clear message format.

8. _____ (behavior)

_____ (interpretation)

_____ (feeling)

_____ (consequence)

_____ (intention)

9. _____ (behavior)

_____ (interpretation)

_____ (feeling)

_____ (consequence)

_____ (intention)

10. _____ (behavior)

_____ (interpretation)

_____ (feeling)

_____ (consequence)

_____ (intention)

9.4 NONDEFENSIVE RESPONSES TO CRITICISM

❖ **Activity Type: Skill Builder**

Purpose

To practice nondefensive responses to typical criticisms you may face.

Instructions

1. For each situation below, write a nondefensive response you could use that follows the guidelines of seeking more information or agreeing with the critic described in Chapter 9 of *Looking Out/Looking In*.
2. Join with two partners and identify the members as A, B, and C.
3. Role-play situations 1 and 2 with A responding to the criticisms offered by B, while C uses 9.5 *Coping with Criticism* to evaluate A's behavior.
4. Switch roles so that B responds to C's criticisms on items 3 and 4, while A completes the checklist.
5. Switch roles again so that C responds to A's criticisms on items 5 and 6, while B completes the checklist.

SITUATION/CRITICISM	EFFECTIVE RESPONSE TO CRITICISM
1. You've been late to work every day this week. Just who do you think you are that you can come wandering in after the rest of us are already working?	
2. This place is a mess! Don't you care about how we live?	
3. You should have consulted somebody before acting on that.	
4. Your sister got terrific grades this term.	

SITUATION/CRITICISM	EFFECTIVE RESPONSE TO CRITICISM
5. How could you have been so thoughtless at the party last night?	
6. Why can't you understand?	
7. You think I'm your personal servant!	
8. Haven't you finished that yet?	
9. You haven't been very affectionate.	
10. I wonder what those parents do to make their children so well-behaved when yours run all over the place.	
11. Criticism of you:	
12. Criticism of you:	

9.5 COPING WITH CRITICISM

❖ Activity Type: Oral Skill

Purpose

To practice nondefensive responses to criticisms.

Instructions

1. Form triads and identify members as A, B, and C. (OR form dyads, videotape the following, and receive evaluation from your instructor)
2. Person A describes a common defensiveness-arousing criticism he or she faces, identifying the critic, topic, and the critic's behavior.
3. Person B paraphrases and questions A until he or she understands the critic's behavior.
4. Persons A and B then role-play the situation, with A practicing the skills of seeking more information and agreeing with the critic as described in Chapter 9 of *Looking Out/Looking In*.
5. Person C uses *Coping with Criticism* to evaluate A's skill at responding nondefensively.
6. After the role-play, person C provides feedback to person A.
7. Rotate roles and repeat steps 1–6 until both B and C have had the chance to practice responding nondefensively to criticism.
8. On a separate page, write a thoughtful, realistically complete assessment of how you used the skills for coping with criticism here, and how you could apply these skills in everyday life.

CHECKLIST

Seeks additional information to understand criticism and critic

—asks for specific details of criticism   _____

—guesses about specific details when critic does not supply facts   _____

—asks what the critic wants   _____

—asks critic to describe the consequences of behavior   _____

("How does my behavior [be specific] cause problems for you?")   _____

—asks what else is wrong   _____

Agrees as appropriate with criticism

—agrees with facts (truth only)   _____

—agrees with critic's right to perceive event differently   _____

("I can understand why it looks that way to you because . . .")   _____

Vocal and nonverbal behaviors
—indicate sincerity (voice, facial expression, posture and gestures, body orientation and distance)
—sound realistic and consistent with speaker's style   _____

                                                    Total   _____

9.6 MEDIATED MESSAGES – CLIMATE

❖ **Activity Type: Group Discussion**

Purpose

To apply the concept of communication climate to mediated contexts.

Instructions

Discuss each of the questions below in your group. Prepare written answers for your instructor, or be prepared to contribute to a large group discussion, comparing your experiences with those of others in your class.

1. Describe how the use of mediated forms of communication channels (e.g., telephone, e-mail) contribute to the communication climate (emotional tone) of your relationships.

   _____

   _____

2. Compile a list of the ways we can use mediated messages to recognize, acknowledge, and endorse others.

   _____

   _____

3. Give examples of how mediated messages have contributed to or helped minimize defensive spirals (negative, ineffective patterns of communication) in your relationships.

   _____

   _____

   _____

4. Your text describes ways we can respond nondefensively to criticism. In which mediated contexts can this skill be used most effectively?

   _____

   _____

5. Go online to RateMyProfessors.com. This is an independent forum in which college students can praise—or, more often, slam—the work of their instructors. Evaluate the confirming and disconfirming aspects of this site.

   _____

   _____

   _____

Chapter Nine

9.6 YOUR CALL – CLIMATE

❖ Activity Type: Group Discussion

Purpose

To analyze defensiveness in relationships.

Instructions

Use the case below and the discussion questions that follow to discuss the variety of communication issues involved in effective communication. Make notes on this page, add other pages on your own, or prepare a group report/analysis based on your discussion. Add your own experiences to individualize the analysis to make it **Your Call**.

Case

Gil and Lydia are brother and sister. They love one another and feel close. Their mother often tells Gil how lovely it is of Lydia to call her so often, how pretty Lydia is, what a good athlete she is, and how much she enjoys Lydia bringing home her friends to visit. Mother tells Lydia how smart Gil is, how hard he works, how many interesting things he does, and how well he manages money. The overall climate of the relationship between Gil and Lydia and their mother is good, but both Gil and Lydia find themselves getting defensive when their mother praises the other.

1. Explain why Gil and Lydia get defensive about these positive statements about the other.

   _____

   _____

   _____

2. Discuss situations similar to the one above in which people get defensive about statements that, on the surface, are positive and supportive.

   _____

   _____

   _____

3. Write coping with criticism responses for Gil or Lydia to use the next time their mother praises their sibling.

   _____

   _____

4. How could Gil and Lydia's mother change the comments she makes about each sibling to reduce defensive reactions?

   _____

   _____

9.8 DEAR PROFESSOR – RELATIONAL RESPONSES

◆❖ Activity Type: Invitation to Insight/Group Discussion

Purposes

1. To examine communication challenges addressed by this chapter.
2. To demonstrate your ability to analyze communication challenges using the concepts in this chapter.

Instructions

Read the Dear Professor letter and response below.
Discuss ProfMary's response. Would you add anything or give a different response?
Read the second letter. Construct an answer to it, <u>using terms and concepts from this chapter.</u>
   <u>Underline or boldface the terms and concepts you apply here.</u>
Before composing your response, use your InfoTrac connection to read *Intimacy development: The influence of abuse and gender*, by Jennifer Ducharme, Catherine Koverola and Paula Battle, in the *Journal of Interpersonal Violence* (1997), volume 12, number 4, pages 590-600. Apply the concepts about trust and violence to your answer.
If class structure permits, share your letters and answers with other members of the class.

Part A - The letter

Dear Professor,

My boss is very critical of my appearance. Every time I see him he has something nasty to say. I'm a security guard, and he thinks I should look more professional. I'm always clean and dressed in my uniform, but he says things like, "When are you going to shave off that beard?" Yesterday, he even told me to stuff my hair under my hat. How can I get him to not sweat the small stuff? **Lee**

The response

Dear Lee,

*I assume your boss is not criticizing your job performance, so the "small stuff" you mention refers to your appearance. Your hair may matter more to him than was apparent when you took the job. And, even when you know you are clean and well-groomed, it is difficult to avoid becoming **defensive** when someone criticizes your appearance.*

*Check your dress code to be sure you are in compliance (pay particular attention to what is proscribed about facial hair or hair length). The next time your boss uses **evaluation** about your appearance, try **coping with the criticism** in a **supportive** way. Try **description** ("My sideburns <u>are</u> one inch below my ear; did you think they were longer?") or **empathy** ("Hmm. Are you worried my hair length is affecting my ability to do my job effectively?").*

*Perhaps you can **get more details** about what is bothering your boss, **agree with whatever is true** (facts only), and then **ask what your boss would like you to do** within the boundaries of your work contract. Keep a positive attitude, indicating sincerity and appreciation for the boss's point of view. You may not solve the problem or get your boss to admit that you are right. You will probably feel less **defensive**, though, if you feel good about the **confirming** way in which you addressed the problem.*

In hopes for your relational satisfaction,   ***ProfMary***

Part B - The letter

Dear Professor,

My best friend was in a relationship with a guy who broke her trust numerous times. How she's in a new relationship with a great guy, but she doesn't trust him. She's constantly sending people to "test" him by kissing him and seeing how he reacts. She has them ask him questions about her and then report back what he says. I don't think this is very healthy, and that she's almost creating a self-fulfilling prophecy that he will break her trust. How can I make her see this? ***Althea***

Your response

Dear Althea,

_____

_____

_____

_____

_____

_____

_____

_____

_____

_____

_____

_____

Study Guide

CHECK YOUR UNDERSTANDING

Crossword Puzzle

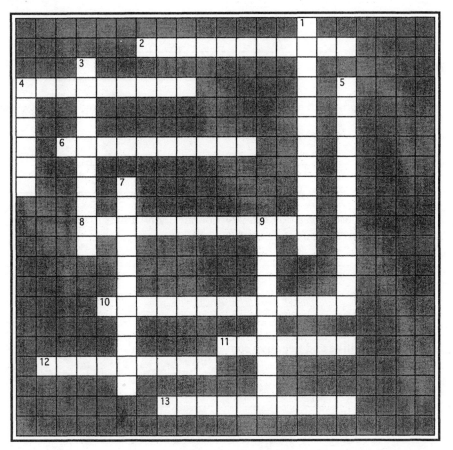

ACROSS

2. communication in which the sender tries to impose some sort of outcome on the receiver, usually resulting in a defensive reaction
4. a disconfirming response with more than one meaning, leaving the other party unsure of the responder's position
6. communication messages that express caring or respect for another person
8. a defense mechanism in which a person stresses a strength in one area to camouflage a shortcoming in some other area
10. communication messages that express a lack of caring or respect for another person
11. the emotional tone of a relationship between two or more individuals
12. an element of a clear message that includes future action plans and requests of others
13. a disconfirming response that is superficial or trite

DOWN

1. a defense mechanism in which a person vents hostile or aggressive feelings on a target that cannot strike back, instead of on the true target
3. a cognitive inconsistency between two conflicting pieces of information, attitudes or behavior
4. a defense mechanism in which a person avoids admitting emotional pain by pretending not to care about an event
5. a disconfirming response in which one communicator breaks into the other's communication
7. a disconfirming response that generally implies a character fault in the other person
9. a disconfirming response that ignores another person's attempt to communicate

True/False

Mark the statements below as true or false. Correct false statements on the lines below to create true statements.

_____ 1. The tone or climate of a relationship is shaped by the degree to which the people believe themselves to be valued by one another.

_____

_____

_____

_____ 2. Disagreeing with another person is always disconfirming or defense-arousing.

_____

_____

_____

_____ 3. Most experts agree that it is psychologically healthier to have someone ignore you than disagree with you.

_____

_____

_____

_____ 4. Both positive and negative communication spirals have their limits; they rarely go on indefinitely.

_____

_____

_____

_____ 5. When the criticism leveled at us is accurate, we will not get defensive.

_____

_____

_____

_____   6. Communicators strive to resolve inconsistencies or conflicting pieces of information because this "dissonant" condition is uncomfortable.

_____

_____

_____

_____   7. Using Jack Gibb's supportive behaviors will eliminate defensiveness in your receivers.

_____

_____

_____

_____   8. According to your text, spontaneity can sometimes be used as a strategy.

_____

_____

_____

_____   9. When you truly understand hostile comments, you just naturally accept them.

_____

_____

_____

_____   10. In order to cope with criticism, you should agree with all the critics' statements.

_____

_____

_____

Completion

The Gibb categories of defensive and supportive behavior are six sets of contrasting styles of verbal and nonverbal behavior. Each set describes a communication style that is likely to arouse defensiveness and a contrasting style that is likely to prevent or reduce it. Fill in the blanks with the Gibb behavior described chosen from the list below.

evaluation	description	control	problem orientation	strategy
spontaneity	neutrality	empathy	superiority	equality
certainty	provisionalism			

1. _____ is the attitude behind messages that dogmatically imply that the speaker's position is correct and that the other person's ideas are not worth considering.

2. _____ is communication behavior involving messages that describe the speaker's position without evaluating others.

3. _____ is a supportive style of communication in which the communicators focus on working together to solve their problems instead of trying to impose their own solutions on one another.

4. _____ is a defense-arousing style of communication in which the sender tries to manipulate or deceive a receiver.

5. _____ is a supportive style of communication in which the sender expresses a willingness to consider the other person's position.

6. _____ is a defense-arousing style of communication in which the sender states or implies that the receiver is not worthy of respect.

7. _____ is a supportive communication behavior in which the sender expresses a message openly and honestly without any attempt to manipulate the receiver.

8. _____ is a defense-arousing behavior in which the sender expresses indifference toward a receiver.

9. _____ is a defense-arousing message in which the sender tries to impose some sort of outcome on the receiver.

10. _____ is a type of supportive communication that suggests that the sender regards the receiver as worthy of respect.

11. _____ is a defense-arousing message in which the sender passes some type of judgment on the receiver.

12. _____ is a type of supportive communication in which the sender accepts the other's feelings as valid and avoids sounding indifferent.

Multiple Choice

Choose the letter of the defensive or supportive category that is best illustrated by each of the situations below.

a. evaluation
b. control
c. strategy
d. neutrality
e. superiority
f. certainty

g. description
h. problem orientation
i. spontaneity
j. empathy
k. equality
l. provisionalism

_____   1. Gerry insists he has all the facts and needs to hear no more information.

_____   2. Richard has a strong opinion but will listen to another position.

_____   3. Lina kept looking at the clock as she was listening to Nan, so Nan thought Lina didn't consider her comments as very important.

_____   4. "I know Janice doesn't agree with me," Mary said, "but she knows how strongly I feel about this, and I think she understands my position."

_____   5. "Even though my professor has a Ph.D.," Rosa pointed out, "she doesn't act like she's the only one who knows something; she is really interested in me as a person."

_____   6. "When I found out that Bob had tricked me into thinking his proposal was my idea so I'd support it, I was really angry."

_____   7. "Even though we *all* wait tables here, Evanne thinks she's better than any of us—just look at the way she prances around!"

_____   8. Clara sincerely and honestly told Georgia about her reservations concerning Georgia's planned party.

_____   9. The co-workers attempted to find a solution to the scheduling issue that would satisfy both of their needs.

_____   10. "It seems as though my father's favorite phrase is 'I know what's best for you' and that really gripes me."

_____   11. "You drink too much."

_____   12. "I was embarrassed when you slurred your speech in front of my boss."

_____   13. "The flowers and presents are just an attempt to get me to go to bed with him."

_____   14. "She looked down her nose at me when I told her I didn't exercise regularly."

_____   15. "Well, if you need more money and I need more help around here, what could we do to make us both happy?"

Choose the letter of the type of coping with criticism that is best illustrated by each of the situations below.
a. ask for specific details of criticism
b. guess about specific details
c. paraphrase to clarify criticism
d. ask what the critic wants
e. ask what else is wrong
f. agree with true facts
g. agree with critic's right to perceive differently

Criticism: "You never seem to care about much."

_____ 16. "Are you referring to my not going to the office party?"

_____ 17. "You're right that I didn't call you back within 24 hours."

_____ 18. "What do you want me to care more about?"

_____ 19. "I can see why you'd be upset with me for not coming to the party because you've told me you want me to be more involved with your work's social events."

_____ 20. "When I didn't come to the party, were you embarrassed or something?"

_____ 21. "So not calling you back right away was a problem. Have I upset you any other way?"

_____ 22. "So you're upset that I'm not visiting you every week, and you think that shows a lack of affection on my part—is that it?"

_____ 23. "What do you mean?"

_____ 24. "You're correct in that I couldn't visit this week because of finals."

_____ 25. "Because I wasn't at the party, it reflected badly on you?"

Identify which element of a clear message is being used in each statement according to the following key:
a. behavioral description
b. interpretation
c. feeling
d. consequence
e. intention

_____ 26. That's a good idea.

_____ 27. I'm worried about this course.

_____ 28. Jim looked angry today.

_____ 29. I want to talk to you about the $20 you borrowed.

_____ 30. I notice that you haven't been smiling much lately.

_____ 31. I don't know whether you're serious or not.

_____ 32. I'm glad you invited me.

_____ 33. Ever since then I've found myself avoiding you.

_____ 34. I'm sorry you didn't like my work.

_____ 35. I want you to know how important this is to me.

_____ 36. It looks to me like you meant to embarrass me.

_____ 37. After the party at Art's, you seemed to withdraw.

_____ 38. I see you're wearing my ring again.

_____ 39. From now on you can count on me.

_____ 40. I've never heard you say a curse word before.

_____ 41. . . . and since then I've been sleeping at my dad's house.

_____ 42. Because that occurred, they won't work overtime.

_____ 43. Dith sighed and looked out the window.

_____ 44. I'm excited about the possibility.

_____ 45. I'll get another place to live.

CHAPTER 9 STUDY GUIDE ANSWERS

Crossword Puzzle

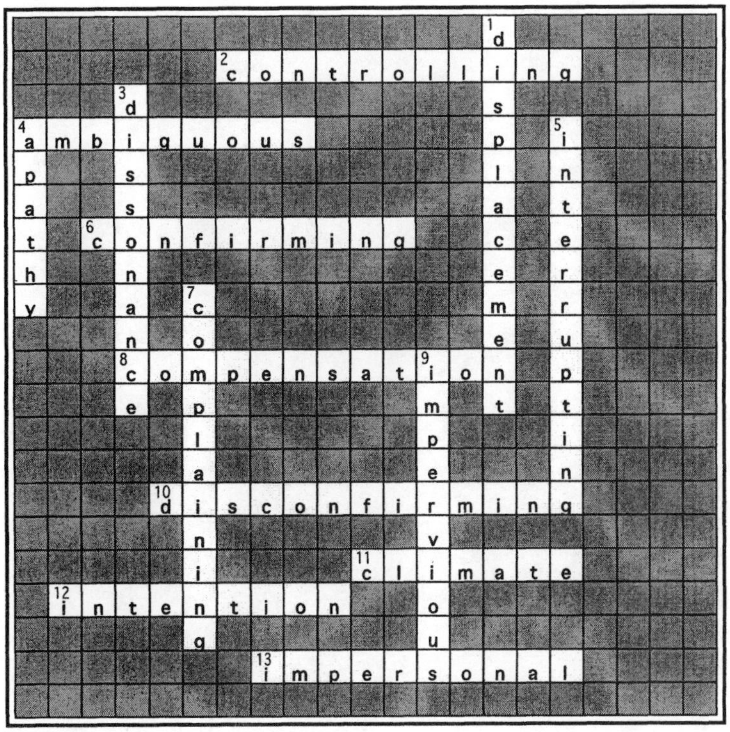

Across:
- 2. controlling
- 4. ambiguous
- 6. confirming
- 8. compensation
- 10. disconfirming
- 11. climate
- 12. intention
- 13. impersonal

Down:
- 1. d
- 3. d
- 5. i

(Crossword grid with the following filled entries:)
- 1 down: **d**isplacement area (d s p l a c e m e n t)
- 2 across: **c**ontrolling
- 3 down: **d**ssessing
- 4 across: **a**mbiguous / 4 down: **a**pathy
- 5 down: **i**nterrupt / **i**nterruption
- 6 across: **c**onfirming / 6 down: **c**nnana
- 7 down: **c**ompensate
- 8 across: **c**ompensation / 8 down: **c**eel... complaining
- 9 down: **i**mpervious
- 10 across: **d**isconfirming
- 11 across: **c**limate / 11 down: **c**lous
- 12 across: **i**ntention
- 13 across: **i**mpersonal

True/False

1. T	3. F	5. F	7. F	9. F
2. F	4. T	6. T	8. T	10. F

Completion

1. certainty
2. description
3. problem orientation
4. strategy
5. provisionalism
6. superiority
7. spontaneity
8. neutrality
9. control
10. equality
11. evaluation
12. empathy

Multiple choice

1. f	10. b	19. g	28. b	37. b
2. l	11. a	20. b	29. e	38. a
3. d	12. g	21. e	30. a	39. e
4. j	13. c	22. c	31. b	40. a
5. k	14. e	23. a	32. c	41. d
6. c	15. h	24. f	33. d	42. d
7. e	16. b	25. b	34. c	43. a
8. I	17. f	26. b	35. e	44. c
9. h	18. d	27. c	36. b	45. e

CHAPTER TEN

MANAGING INTERPERSONAL CONFLICTS

OUTLINE

Use this outline to take notes as you read the chapter in the text and/or as your instructor lectures in class.

I. **THE NATURE OF CONFLICT**
   A. **Definition**
      1. Expressed struggle
      2. Perceived incompatible goals
      3. Perceived scarce rewards
      4. Interdependence
      5. Interference from the other party
   B. **Conflict Is Natural**
   C. **Conflict Can Be Beneficial**

II. **PERSONAL CONFLICT STYLES**
   A. **Nonassertive Behavior**
      1. Avoidance
      2. Accommodation
   B. **Direct Aggression**
   C. **Passive Aggression - "Crazymaking"**
   D. **Indirect Communication**
   E. **Assertion**
   F. **Determining the Best Style**
      1. Situation
      2. Receiver
      3. Your goals

III. **CONFLICT IN RELATIONAL SYSTEMS**
   A. **Complementary, Symmetrical, and Parallel Styles**
   B. **Intimate and Aggressive Styles**
   C. **Conflict Rituals**

IV. **VARIABLES IN CONFLICT STYLES**
   A. **Gender**
      1. Socialization
      2. Situation

   B. **Culture**
      1. Individualism versus collectivism
      2. Low-context versus high-context
      3. Ethnicity
      4. Biology and environment

V. **METHODS OF CONFLICT RESOLUTION**
   A. **Win–Lose**
   B. **Lose–Lose**
   C. **Compromise**
   D. **Win–Win**

VI. **WIN–WIN COMMUNICATION SKILLS**
   A. **Identify Your Problem and Unmet Needs**
   B. **Make a Date**
   C. **Describe Your Problem and Needs**
   D. **Consider Your Partner's Point of View**
   E. **Negotiate a Solution**
      1. Identify and define the conflict
      2. Generate a number of possible solutions
      3. Evaluate the alternative solutions
      4. Decide on the best solution
   F. **Follow Up the Solution**

VII. **CONSTRUCTIVE CONFLICT: QUESTIONS AND ANSWERS**
   A. **Isn't Win–Win Too Good to Be True?**
   B. **Isn't Win–Win Too Elaborate?**
   C. **Isn't Win–Win Negotiating *Too* Rational?**
   D. **Is It Possible to Change Others?**

KEY TERMS

assertion
avoidance
complementary conflict style
compromise
conflict
conflict ritual
crazymaking
direct aggression
indirect communication

lose-lose problem solving
nonassertion
parallel conflict style
passive aggression
relational conflict style
symmetrical conflict style
win-lose problem solving
win-win problem solving

ACTIVITIES

10.1 UNDERSTANDING CONFLICT STYLES

◆❖ **Activity Type: Skill Builder**

Purpose

To understand the styles with which conflicts can be handled.

Instructions

1. For each of the conflicts described below, write four responses illustrating nonassertive, directly aggressive, passive aggressive, indirect communication, and assertive communication styles.
2. Describe the probable consequences of each style.

Example

Three weeks ago your friend borrowed an article of clothing, promising to return it soon. You haven't seen it since, and the friend hasn't mentioned it.

Nonassertive response *Say nothing to the friend, hoping she will remember and return the item.*

Probable consequences *There's a good chance I'll never get the item back. I would probably resent the friend and avoid her in the future so I won't have to lend anything else.*

Directly aggressive response *Confront the friend and accuse her of being inconsiderate and irresponsible. Say that she probably ruined the item and is afraid to say so.*

Probable consequences *My friend would get defensive and hurt. Even if she did intentionally keep the item, she'd never admit it when approached this way. We would probably avoid each other in the future.*

Passive aggressive response *Complain to another friend, knowing it will get back to her.*

Probable consequences *My friend might be embarrassed by my gossip and be even more resistant to return it.*

Indirect communication *Drop hints about how I loved to wear the borrowed item. Casually mention how much I hate people who don't return things.*

Probable consequences *My friend might ignore my hints. She'll most certainly resent my roundabout approach, even if she returns the article.*

Assertive response *Confront the friend in a noncritical way and remind her that she still has the item. Ask when she'll return it, being sure to get a specific time.*

Probable consequences *The friend might be embarrassed when I bring the subject up, but since there's no attack it'll probably be okay. Since we'll have cleared up the problem, the relationship can continue.*

1. Someone you've just met at a party criticizes a mutual friend in a way you think is unfair.

    Nonassertive response _____

    _____

Probable consequences _____

_____

Directly aggressive response _____

_____

Probable consequences _____

_____

Passive aggressive response _____

_____

Probable consequences _____

_____

Indirect communication _____

_____

Probable consequences _____

_____

Assertive response _____

_____

Probable consequences _____

_____

2. A fan behind you at a ballgame toots a loud air horn every time the home team makes any progress. The noise is spoiling your enjoyment of the game.

Nonassertive response _____

_____

Probable consequences _____

_____

Directly aggressive response _____

_____

Class _____ Name _____

Probable consequences _____

_____

Passive aggressive response _____

_____

Probable consequences _____

_____

Indirect communication _____

_____

Probable consequences _____

_____

Assertive response _____

_____

Probable consequences _____

_____

3. Earlier in the day you asked the person with whom you live to stop by the store and pick up snacks for a party you are having this evening. Your roommate arrives home without the food, and it's too late to return to the store.

Nonassertive response _____

_____

Probable consequences _____

_____

Directly aggressive response _____

_____

Probable consequences _____

_____

Passive aggressive response _____

_____

Probable consequences _____

Indirect communication _____

_____

Probable consequences _____

_____

Assertive response _____

_____

Probable consequences _____

_____

4. You are explaining your political views to a friend who has asked your opinion. Now the friend obviously isn't listening. You think to yourself that since the person asked for your ideas, the least he or she can do is pay attention.

Nonassertive response _____

_____

Probable consequences _____

_____

Directly aggressive response _____

_____

Probable consequences _____

_____

Passive aggressive response _____

_____

Probable consequences _____

_____

Indirect communication _____

_____

Probable consequences _____

_____

Class _____ Name _____

Assertive response _____

_____

Probable consequences _____

_____

5. You find out that a friend at work told other people with whom you work some very personal information about you.

Nonassertive response _____

_____

Probable consequences _____

_____

Directly aggressive response _____

_____

Probable consequences _____

_____

Passive aggressive response _____

_____

Probable consequences _____

_____

Indirect communication _____

_____

Probable consequences _____

_____

Assertive response _____

_____

Probable consequences _____

_____

_____

_____

10.2 YOUR CONFLICT STYLES

◆ **Activity Type: Invitation to Insight**

Purpose

To identify the styles you use to handle conflicts.

Instructions

1. Use the form below to record the conflicts that occur in your life. Describe any minor issues that arise as well as major problems.
2. For each incident, describe your conflict style, your approach to resolution, and the consequences of these behaviors.
3. Summarize your findings in the space provided.

INCIDENT	YOUR BEHAVIOR	YOUR CONFLICT STYLE	APPROACH TO RESOLUTION	CONSEQUENCES
Example My friend accused me of being too negative about the possibility of finding rewarding, well-paying work.	I became defensive and angrily denied his claim. In turn I accused him of being too critical.	Direct aggression	Win-lose	After arguing for some time, we left each other, both feeling upset. I'm sure we'll both feel awkward around each other for a while.
1.				
2.				
3.				

INCIDENT	YOUR BEHAVIOR	YOUR CONFLICT STYLE	APPROACH TO RESOLUTION	CONSEQUENCES
4.				
5.				

Conclusions

Are there any individuals or issues that repeatedly arouse conflicts?

_____

_____

What conflict style(s) do you most commonly use? Do you use different styles with different people or in different situations? Describe.

_____

_____

_____

_____

_____

_____

What approaches do you usually take in resolving conflicts? Do you use different approaches depending on the people or situations? Describe.

_____

_____

_____

What are the consequences of the behaviors you described above? Are you satisfied with them? If not, how could you change?

_____

_____

_____

_____

Through your InfoTrac connection, read about conflict and the aftermath of divorce: *Managing conflict after marriages end: A qualitative study of narratives of ex-spouses* by Susan Walzer and Thomas P. Oles, (2003). *Families in Society: The Journal of Contemporary Human Services*, volume 84, issue 2, 192-201. How can you apply what you know about conflict to the particular challenges these people face?

_____

_____

_____

_____

Chapter Ten

10.3 THE END VS. THE MEANS

◆❖ Activity Type: Invitation to Insight

Purpose

To distinguish the ends from the means in a personal conflict.

Instructions

1. In each of the conflict situations below, identify the <u>ends</u> each party seems to be seeking. There may be ends that the relationship shares as well as individual ends for each of the parties involved. Ends in a conflict are the overall, general (often relational) goals that the dyad has.
2. Brainstorm a series of possible <u>means</u> that could achieve each person's (and the relationship's) ends. Means are the many possible ways to reach the end state.
3. Record conflict situations of your own, identifying ends and means.

CONFLICT SITUATION	SHARED ENDS	SPEAKER'S ENDS	OTHER'S ENDS	POSSIBLE MEANS
Example My friend wants me to visit her in Washington and meet her family. I'd like to visit, but it would cost a lot, and I'd rather save the money for something else.	We both want to maintain the affection in the relationship. We both want one another to know we are important to one another and that we care about one another and our families.	I want to spend as little money as possible while still letting my friend know how important she is to me. I don't want to lose her friendship.	She wants to show her family what a good friend I am and have some companionship while she has to stay in Washington.	She/her family sends me money to go to Washington. We share the cost. I combine whatever else I want to do with a short trip to Washington. We arrange for the family to meet me when they next come to our city. My friend comes back with her sister or mother to spend time with me.
1. My roommate wants a friend (whom I dislike) to sublease a room in our apartment.				

Managing Interpersonal Conflicts

CONFLICT SITUATION	SHARED ENDS	SPEAKER'S ENDS	OTHER'S ENDS	POSSIBLE MEANS
2. I'm dating a person who's of a different race than I am, and my family thinks this is a mistake.				
3. My older sister thinks that I'll turn into an alcoholic when I have a few beers (there are a few alcohol problems in our family). I tell her not to worry, but she won't get off my case.				
4. My mom keeps asking me about my grades and nagging me on the issue of my boyfriend. She thinks I'm going to make the same mistakes as she did.				
5. Some people in my office listen to country music all day. I've got nothing against it, but it gets old. I'd like more variety.				
6. Your example:				

10.4 WIN-WIN PROBLEM SOLVING

◆❖ Activity Type: Invitation to Insight

Purpose

To help you apply the win–win problem-solving method to a personal conflict.

Instructions

1. Follow the instructions below as a guide to dealing with an interpersonal conflict facing you now.
2. After completing the no-lose steps, record your conclusions in the space provided.

Step 1: Identify your unmet needs (i.e., the situation, the person(s) involved, the history, etc.).

_____

_____

Step 2: Make a date. (Choose a time and place that will make it easiest for both parties to work constructively on the issue.)

_____

Step 3: Describe your problem and needs (behavior, interpretation, feeling, consequence, intention) Avoid proposing specific means or solutions at this point.

_____

_____

_____

_____

Step 3A: Ask your partner to show that s/he understandings you (paraphrase or perception-check).

_____

_____

Step 3B: Solicit your partner's point of view/clear message (behavior, interpretation, feeling, consequence, intention).

_____

_____

_____

_____

Step 4: Clarify your partner's point of view (paraphrase or perception-check as necessary).

_____

_____

Step 5: Negotiate a solution.

   a. Restate the needs of both parties (what both have in common).

_____

_____

   b. Work together to generate a number of possible solutions that might satisfy these needs. Don't criticize any suggestions here!

_____

_____

_____

_____

_____

_____

   c. Evaluate the solutions you just listed, considering the advantages and problems of each. If you think of any new solutions, record them above.

_____

_____

_____

   d. Decide on the best solution, listing it here.

_____

_____

Step 6: Follow up the solution. Set a trial period, and then plan to meet with your partner and see if your agreement is satisfying both your needs. If not, return to step 3 and use this procedure to refine your solution.

_____

_____

Conclusions

In what ways did this procedure differ from the way in which you usually deal with interpersonal conflicts?

_____

_____

_____

Was the outcome of your problem-solving session different from what it might have been if you had communicated in your usual style? How?

_____

_____

_____

_____

In what ways can you use the no-lose methods in your interpersonal conflicts? With whom? On what issues? What kinds of behavior will be especially important?

_____

_____

_____

_____

10.5 CONFLICT RESOLUTION DYADS

❖ Activity Type: Oral Skill

Purpose

To develop your skills in using the assertive, win–win conflict resolution methods introduced in Chapter 10 of *Looking Out/Looking In.*

Instructions

1. Join with a partner and discuss conflicts from your lives. Choose one that would be suitable for a win-win conflict attempt. One of you will role-play a real life partner.
2. Engage in the win–win conflict resolution methods introduced in Chapter 10 of *Looking Out/Looking In.* (You may use 10.4 to help you prepare this conflict.)
3. Use the *Checklist* below to evaluate your performance (or videotape the conflict dyad and evaluate one another's performance).
4. On a separate sheet of paper, evaluate your performance in this dyad, and describe how this method can be effectively and realistically applied to everyday conflicts.

Set a "date" for discussing the issue _____

Describes unmet needs to partner _____
   —other's behavior _____
   —your interpretations _____
   —your feelings _____
   —consequences (for self and/or other) _____
   —intentions _____

Seeks verification that partner understands statement of needs _____

Solicits partner's needs, as appropriate _____

Actively listens/perception checks to verify understanding of partner's needs _____

Negotiates win–win solution to best possible extent _____
   —identifies/summarizes conflict _____
   —generates possible solutions without criticizing _____
   —evaluates alternatives _____
   —decides on win–win solution _____

Plans follow-up meeting to modify solution as necessary. _____

Describes how this method can be applied to everyday conflicts _____

TOTAL ___

10.6 MEDIATED MESSAGES – CONFLICT MANAGEMENT

❖ **Activity Type: Group Discussion**

Purpose

To manage conflict in mediated contexts.

Instructions

Discuss each of the questions below in your group. Prepare written answers for your instructor, or be prepared to contribute to a large group discussion, comparing your experiences with those of others in your class.

1. Describe how conflict can occur in mediated contexts (e.g. e-mail, instant messaging/chat, telephone, and hard copy). Describe how you might manage conflict using mediated communication channels.

_____

_____

_____

2. Describe how mediated communication channels might help or hinder the brainstorming process (an important aspect of win-win problem-solving).

_____

_____

_____

3. Describe gender and/or cultural differences in conflict management that might occur in mediated contexts.

_____

_____

_____

4. Go online to http://jeffcoweb.jeffco.k12.co.us/high/wotc/confli1.htm and take a brief quiz about your approaches to conflict (are you a turtle, shark, bear, fox, or owl?). After you score yourself (most common conflict style and the second--most usually used under stress), comment below on how a mediated situation might alter your conflict style(s).

_____

_____

_____

10.7 YOUR CALL – CONFLICT MANAGEMENT

❖ **Activity Type: Group Discussion**

Purpose

To apply conflict management principles to a relationship.

Instructions

Use the case below and the discussion questions that follow to discuss the variety of communication issues involved in effective communication. Make notes on this page, add other pages on your own, or prepare a group report/analysis based on your discussion. Add your own experiences to individualize the analysis to make it **Your Call**.

Case

Klaus and Drew have been roommates for two years, and they have had very few problems. But this term Klaus has a difficult and early class schedule, and he has taken on more hours at work to make ends meet. Drew's parents support him completely and he has a very light schedule this term. Klaus and Drew's friends continue to come to their house to party, and Drew is very irritated with Klaus because he's always studying and is a big bore all of a sudden. Klaus thinks Drew is a spoiled brat and insensitive to his needs. Neither Klaus nor Drew has said anything at this point.

1. Should Klaus and Drew bring this conflict out in the open? Would airing their differences be beneficial or harmful to the relationship?

   _____

   _____

   _____

2. What are the unmet needs of Klaus and Drew in this situation? Should they keep those unmet needs to themselves (be unassertive) or should they use one of the other personal conflict styles?

   _____

   _____

   _____

3. Evaluate the potential of the win-win problem-solving method to solve this situation.

   _____

   _____

   _____

10.8 DEAR PROFESSOR – RELATIONAL RESPONSES

◆❖ **Activity Type: Invitation to Insight/Group Discussion**

Purposes

1. To examine communication challenges addressed by this chapter.
2. To demonstrate your ability to analyze communication challenges using the concepts in this chapter.

Instructions

1. Read the Dear Professor letter and response below.
2. Discuss ProfMary's response. Would you add anything or give a different response?
3. Read the second letter. Construct an answer to it, <u>using terms and concepts from this chapter.</u> <u>Underline or boldface the terms and concepts you apply here.</u>
4. If class structure permits, share your letters and answers with other members of the class.

Part A - The letter

Dear Professor,

My brother has a dog, and it's not my responsibility, but I have to care for it many times because my brother doesn't do what he should. I try telling my brother that he should clean up after the dog and take it out when it needs it, but he still seems to think that I should take some responsibility since we live together. I don't want to have any responsibility for this dog. How can I make my brother realize that he is responsible for his dog? **Lupe**

The response

Dear Lupe,

*You probably want to maintain a positive relationship with your brother, so you need a **problem-orientation** approach to this situation that will meet as many of the **needs** of you and your brother as possible. You both need to **assert** your wants and needs to one another concerning the dog and your living situation.*

*First, approach your brother with an **intimate-nonaggressive style** that minimizes attacking and blaming. Assert that you value your relationship with your brother and that you want what is best for both of you. Use the **clear message format** to express the whole range of your thoughts and feelings about how often you do things for the dog, what you think about it, and how you feel. Then solicit the thoughts and feelings of your brother.*

*Brainstorm a list of options that could fit each of your needs (don't evaluate them to start with). Then combine, rearrange, or eliminate various options until you come up with one(s) that might work. **Decide on the solution**, establish a trial period, and then agree to **check back** if the solution isn't working. Aim for a **win-win solution**, but realize that **compromise** might also meet your needs as you define them. Remember that maintaining the relationship between you and your brother is a very important factor.*

In hopes for your relational satisfaction,   **ProfMary**

Part B - The letter

Dear Professor,

I have a good friend who lives in another city. He comes to visit me, which I like, but he sometimes stays for three weeks and eats my food and wears my clothes. I feel taken advantage of, even though I enjoy his company. How can I tell him without jeopardizing the friendship? **Vincente**

Your response

Dear Vincente,

_____

_____

_____

_____

_____

_____

_____

_____

_____

_____

_____

Study Guide

CHECK YOUR UNDERSTANDING

Crossword Puzzle

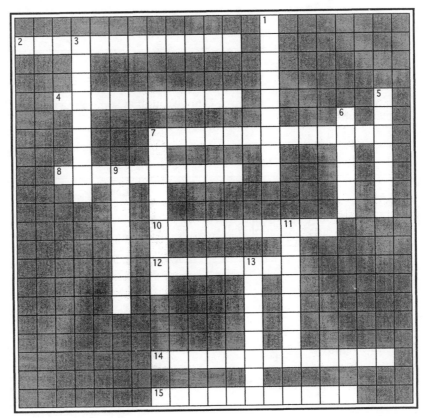

ACROSS

2. the inability to express one's thoughts or feelings when necessary
4. a conflict style that is a pattern of managing disagreements that repeats itself over time in a relationship
7. a nonassertive response style in which the communicator submits to a situation rather than attempt to have his or her needs met
8. an approach to conflict resolution in which both parties attain at least part of what they wanted through self-sacrifice
10. a criticism or demand that threatens the face of the person to whom it is directed
12. an expressed struggle between at least two interdependent parties who perceive incompatible goals, scarce rewards, and interference
14. a relational conflict style in which partners use different but mutually reinforcing behaviors
15. a relational conflict style in which both partners use the same tactics

DOWN

1. an approach to conflict resolution in which neither side achieves its goals
3. a direct expression of the sender's needs, thoughts, or feelings, delivered in a way that does not attack the receiver's dignity
5. an approach to conflict resolution in which the parties work together to satisfy all their goals
6. an unacknowledged repeating pattern of interlocking behavior used by participants in a conflict
7. a nonassertive response style in which the communicator is unwilling to confront a situation in which his or her needs are not being met
9. a relational conflict style in which the approach of the partners varies from one situation to another
11. conflict styles that focus on the relational goals
13. communication that is an oblique way of expressing wants or needs in order to save face for the recipient

Managing Interpersonal Conflicts

True/False

Mark the statements below as true or false. Correct statements that are false on the lines below to create a true statement.

_____ 1. A conflict can exist only when both parties are aware of a disagreement.

_____

_____

_____

_____ 2. Conflict will occur only if there is not enough of something (money, love, respect, time, etc.) to go around.

_____

_____

_____

_____ 3. Very close and compatible relationships will not involve conflict.

_____

_____

_____

_____ 4. Effective communication during conflicts can actually keep good relationships strong.

_____

_____

_____

_____ 5. Nonassertion is always a bad idea.

_____

_____

_____

_____ 6. Verbally abusive couples report significantly less relational satisfaction than do partners who communicate about their conflicts in other ways.

_____

_____

_____

_____   7. Assertion is clearly superior to other conflict styles.

_____

_____

_____

_____   8. Crazymaking is just another name for passive aggression.

_____

_____

_____

_____   9. "It takes two to tango"—in conflict, as in dancing, men and women behave in similar ways.

_____

_____

_____

_____   10. The most important cultural factor in shaping attitudes toward conflict is gender.

_____

_____

_____

Completion

Fill in the blanks with the crazymaker term described below.

avoiders   pseudoaccomodators   guiltmakers   subject changers   distracters
mind readers   trivial tyranizers   gunnysackers   beltliners   trappers

1. _____ don't respond immediately when they get angry. Instead, they let conflicts build up until they all pour out at once.

2. _____ do things they know will irritate their conflict partner rather than honestly sharing their resentments.

3. _____ engage in character analyses, explaining what the other person *really* means, instead of allowing their partners to express feelings honestly.

4. _____ set up a desired behavior for their partners and then when the behavior is met, they attack the very thing they requested.

5. _____ refuse to fight by leaving, falling asleep, or pretending to be busy.

6. _____ try to make their partners feel responsible for causing their pain even though they won't come right out and say what they feel or want.

7. _____ refuse to face up to a conflict either by giving in or by pretending that there's nothing at all wrong.

8. _____ use intimate knowledge of their partners to get them "where it hurts."

9. _____ attack other parts of their partner's life rather than express their feelings about the object of their dissatisfaction.

10. _____ escape facing up to aggression by shifting the conversation whenever it approaches an area of conflict.

Multiple Choice

Match the terms below with their definitions.
a. an indirect expression of aggression, delivered in a way that allows the sender to maintain a façade of kindness
b. an oblique way of expressing wants or needs in order to save face for the recipient
c. an uncontrolled, spontaneous explosion involved in conflict
d. an approach to conflict resolution in which one party reaches its goal at the expense of the other
e. a pattern of managing disagreements that repeats itself over time in a relationship

_____ 1. win-lose

_____ 2. indirect communication

_____ 3. "Vesuvius"

_____ 4. conflict style

_____ 5. passive aggression

Choose the letter of the personal conflict style that is best illustrated by the behavior found below.
a. avoidance
b. accommodation
c. direct aggression
d. assertion
e. indirect communication
f. passive aggression

_____ 6. Stan keeps joking around to keep us from talking about commitment.

_____ 7. "I can't believe you were so stupid as to have erased the disk."

_____ 8. Even though he wanted to go to the party, Allen stayed home with Sara rather than hear her complain.

_____ 9. By mentioning how allergic she was to smoke, Joan hoped that her guest would smoke outside.

_____ 10. "When you smoke inside, I start to cough and my eyes water, so please go out on the balcony when you want to smoke."

_____ 11. Rather than tell Nick about his frustration over Nick's not meeting the deadline, Howard complained to others about Nick's unreliability while maintaining a smiling front to Nick.

_____ 12. Carol wouldn't answer the phone after their disagreement because she was afraid it would be Nancy on the other end.

_____ 13. Faced with his obvious distress, Nikki put her very important work aside to listen to him.

_____ 14. Even though Nikki could see Kham's distress, she told him she had a deadline to meet in one hour and asked if they could talk then.

_____ 15. (Sarcastically) "Oh, sure, I *loved* having dinner with your parents instead of going to the party Saturday night."

Choose the best answer for each statement below.

16. When partners use different but mutually reinforcing behaviors, they illustrate a

    a. complementary conflict style
    b. symmetrical conflict style
    c. parallel conflict style
    d. supportive conflict style

17. When both partners in a conflict use the same kinds of conflict behaviors, we say they have a _____ conflict style.

    a. complementary
    b. symmetrical
    c. parallel
    d. supportive

18. Partners who fight but are unsuccessful at satisfying important content and relational goals have a _____ style.

    a. intimate-aggressive
    b. intimate-nonaggressive
    c. nonintimate-nonaggressive
    d. nonintimate-aggressive

19. Partners who avoid conflicts—and one another—instead of facing issues head-on have a _____ style.

    a. intimate-aggressive
    b. intimate-nonaggressive
    c. nonintimate-nonaggressive
    d. nonintimate-aggressive

20. Partners who have a low amount of attacking or blaming, who confront one another either directly or indirectly, but manage to prevent issues from interfering with their relationship have a _____ style.

    a. intimate-aggressive
    b. intimate-nonaggressive
    c. nonintimate-nonaggressive
    d. nonintimate-aggressive

Chapter Ten

CHAPTER 10 STUDY GUIDE ANSWERS

Crossword Puzzle

										¹l						
²n	o	³n	a	s	s	e	r	t	i	o	n					
		s								s						
		s								e					⁵w	
	⁴r	e	l	a	t	i	o	n	a	l			⁶r		i	
	r	t			⁷a	c	c	o	m	m	o	d	a	t	i	o	n
	t		v			s			t				w	
⁸c	o	m	⁹p	r	o	m	i	s	e		e			u		i
	n		a			i						a		n
	r		d		¹⁰a	g	g	r	e	s	s	¹¹i	o	n		
	a		n								n			
	l		¹²c	o	n	f	¹³l	i	c	t				
	l		e				n		i				
	l						d		m				
							i		a				
							r		t				
	¹⁴c	o	m	p	l	e	m	e	n	t	a	r	y
							c						
	¹⁵s	y	m	m	e	t	r	i	c	a	l		

True/False

1. T	3. F	5. F	7. F	9. F
2. F	4. T	6. T	8. T	10. F

Completion

1. gunnysackers
2. trivial tyranizers
3. mind readers
4. trappers
5. avoiders
6. guiltmakers
7. pseudoaccomodators
8. beltliners
9. distractors
10. subject changers

Multiple choice

1. d	5. a	9. e	13. b	17. b
2. b	6. a	10. d	14. d	18. d
3. c	7. c	11. f	15. f	19. c
4. e	8. b	12. a	16. a	20. b